Kindergarten: A Sourcebook
for
School and Home

Janet Rose

DALE SEYMOUR PUBLICATIONS

Acknowledgements

I wish to thank Dr. Carol Plaisted, who graciously allowed me to include several of her activities in this handbook. I also wish to thank Prudy Minich, who developed the activities for the physical education portion of Chapter Three.

Finally, I wish to thank:
Dr. Violet Robinson, for her advice and guidance.
Alan B. Myers, for his continued professional support.
Susan Bellavita, for giving me the original inspiration for this handbook.
Steven Hirsch, for his patient editing, love, and understanding.

Order number DS07405
ISBN 0-86651-212-8

cdefgh-MA-9543210

Dear Teacher,

This *Sourcebook* is at your disposal to duplicate for your classroom parents. How many pages, in what order, and at what point in the year you hand them out depends on your needs and the needs of your parents. The entire book could be duplicated and handed out at one time, or selected activities might be given out as the need arises. For example, some parents have mentioned that it would be useful to have the entire *Sourcebook* the summer before their children enter kindergarten. In that way they could do activities early to prepare their children for school. Other parents might want to have only carefully selected activities that use skills their child needs extra work on. In the past, I have always duplicated the entire sourcebook for my classroom parents. I encourage you to experiment with a variety of methods, and I would greatly appreciate hearing from you (by way of the publisher) regarding what has worked for you. The following guidelines should prove successful no matter which method of duplication you use.

Chapters One and Two should be read by all your parents early in the year so that they have a chance to digest the information before the first parent-teacher conference. The rest of the book could be given to your parents at that time or later, during the first parent-teacher conference.

For the first parent-teacher conference, prepare a list of 6–12 suggested skill areas from the *Sourcebook* for each parent. These skill areas should be chosen for each child based on the child's strengths and weaknesses in the different subject areas. Explain to the parents why you suggest the skill areas as a regular part of your conference ("I listed the skills of left-to-right progression and letter writing because David has difficulty with our handwriting lessons. I would like to see David try some of the science activities because he has shown interest and aptitude in that subject.") Parents can then return home from the conference with a concrete plan of action. Once they have a list of skill areas, they can look in Index II to find appropriate activities. These suggestions take very little time to do, and the parents greatly appreciate the personal effort you have made on behalf of each child. It might be a good idea at this time to give each parent a copy of the letter to the parent and the handwriting and number forms in the appendices.

If you hold two conferences in the year, you may want to make up a second list of suggestions based on the child's progress. In this way, you do not need to give the parents a huge list all at once, as it can be overwhelming. If you do not hold a second conference, a second list can be sent home in letter form sometime in March.

Although all of your parents should read Chapters One and Two, it is important to remember that not all will have the interest and/or the time to carry out the activities. I have not yet found a definite pattern of use—working parents will find the time if they have the interest; non-working parents who do not have the interest will not carry out the activities despite their available time.

This *Sourcebook* will provide the most benefit if you are thoroughly familiar with its contents. Feel free to use it in any way that best suits the families that you serve.

Sincerely,
Janet Rose

Dear Parents,

The purpose of this *Sourcebook* is two-fold: 1) to acquaint you with the kindergarten program, and 2) to provide you with a variety of activities that you can do at home to reinforce and strengthen the concepts and skills taught at school. For the most part, the activities are specific to your child's kindergarten experience. However, the techniques suggested for making the time spent with your child a more intensive learning experience can be applied throughout his* younger years.

The activities are designed to be easily assembled and of high interest to your child. Some of the activities consist of playing a game. Some of them will require a more formal lesson format. Many of the activities can be done during potentially unused times, such as waiting in line, shopping, driving, etc. These less structured activities can often give you much more insight into your child than a more structured lesson-practice session. This type of activity can be developed and changed to challenge your child as he grows.

The format of each activity is as follows. The number and title of the activity are followed by a list of the general skills or concepts covered by the activity. Next comes a specific purpose, or goal, of the activity. Then comes the situation in which the activity takes place, such as when working in the kitchen, travelling in the car, or during leisure time at home. Finally, a list of the materials you will need and the directions for the activity itself are provided. Many of the activities also contain variations that you may try. These were included to meet the needs of the different interests and ability levels of kindergarten children.

Do not feel that you must try all the activities suggested, but choose those that suit your schedule and your child's interests. Repetition of productive activities is important. Feel free to change, modify, or expand the activities to suit your needs.

During parent-teacher conferences, your teacher may suggest specific activities tailored to your child's needs and interests. You are, of course, encouraged to try other activities as well that you feel you and your child would enjoy. The activities suggested for the Social Studies/Science/Health and Art/Music/Drama subject areas work especially well for those long, rainy-day afternoons. Experiment and enjoy!

CONTENTS

Chapter One: The Kindergarten Program

Kindergarten is generally thought of as a year of orientation and transition. For some children, it is their first formal experience away from home and family. For their parents, it can be a first encounter with a particular school—its people, programs, and procedures. However, because of changing social and educational patterns, more and more kindergarten-age children have spent one or more years in a preschool or day care setting. Today's kindergarten classroom must provide a program that satisfies the needs and interests of children from a wide variety of backgrounds.

Kindergarten-age children are at a transitional, but most charming stage in life. They are beginning to achieve independence in self-help skills—tying shoes, crossing streets, and running errands. Socially, they are discovering that other children can be friends to make and keep, rather than someone to merely play alongside. For the most part, friendships can change and re-form as often as every few days, but there is a beginning interest in developing and maintaining long-lasting relationships.

Physically, children at this age grow more coordinated with each passing day. As the body proportions begin to even out, kindergarten children discover the joy in coordinating rhythmic movements such as running, skipping, climbing, bike riding, and rope jumping.

Academically, five-year-olds are entering a period of intense intellectual interest and change. They are constantly taking in information from the environment and working at making order and sense out of the things they see. Kindergarten children still see the world as an often magical place, where pretending to be a lion is almost the same as being a lion. Because they have not yet acquired an adult's capacity for logic, to young children, almost anything is possible! This is a trait to be encouraged, not repressed. To learn about lions, a child may roar, walk like a lion, and pretend to hunt. Only after seeing lions, acting like lions, and reading about lions, will the child fully understand what a lion is.

In kindergarten, children are also in the process of discovering that the printed word is no longer the mystery it once was. Learning to recognize letters and words gives the child access to a whole new world, allowing her more power, self-confidence, and independence.

A well-rounded kindergarten program should provide activities that stimulate all aspects of your child's development. The children's own interests should also be taken into consideration by the teacher when establishing curriculum. As a means of organization, I have divided the program into 10 components under 6 headings. These are: Language Arts, Mathematics, Social Studies/Science/Health, Art/Music/Drama, Physical Education, and Social Development. These components are by no means separate entities, although they are often treated as such. A good program (at any grade level) will try to integrate the subject areas as often as possible in order to make them relevant and interesting.

LANGUAGE ARTS

Language arts is a very broad category, covering everything from speaking to reading to writing. It is the easiest subject area to integrate into the others, because language is so much a part of everything we do. Kindergarten-age children are wonderfully receptive to language arts activities of all kinds. Perhaps the most familiar language arts activity is story time. One of the greatest benefits derived from story time is the enrichment of a child's store of experiences upon which he bases future knowledge. At the same time, his vocabulary is enlarged. Listening to stories—whether read from a book, generated from a felt board, or simply made up on the spot—promotes the concept of plot and character development. Understanding the need for a beginning, middle, and end to a story will help your child as he begins to write on his own. Young children also adore playing with words. Poetry, rhyming, and word games are a natural part of the language arts curriculum.

The aforementioned skills are often classified as "reading readiness" skills. Essentially, they are broadening your child's understanding and use of language. Other reading readiness skills include letter name recognition, letter sound recognition, letter writing, left-right progression, visual and auditory memory, visual and auditory discrimination, and visual-motor coordination.

There continues to be a controversy over the teaching of letter names versus letter sounds. Practically speaking, being able to hear and identify letter sounds is more important in the acquisition of initial reading skills than being able to name the letters. When a child sees the written word *cat,* being able to say "see-ay-tee" does not help him decode the word nearly as much as sounding out "k-a-t." This is not to say that knowing the alphabet is useless. This knowledge makes working with letters more familiar to your child. The least confusing way to approach letters is to tell your child that letters have a name and a sound, which may be different from each other. To really know the letter, you must know both the name and the sound, just as you would know a friend's first and last name.

This leads us to another controversy which concerns the best way to teach beginning reading. Traditionally, the dispute has been over the sight word, or "look-say" approach (popularized by the Dick and Jane series), or the phonics approach. The look-say method relies on memory and repetition to learn whole words, with little emphasis given to the sounds the letters make. The phonics approach, strictly speaking, requires the learning of many letter sounds so that a word is read by breaking it down into its component sounds and blending them together, or "sounding it out." Today's reading series usually combine these approaches with many other equally useful techniques. In general, most kindergarteners are expected to know their letter names and letter sounds, and possibly a few basic words upon entering first grade.

Writing has come to play an important role in the kindergarten curriculum. It is usually done in the form of dictation, whereby the child tells a story to the teacher who records it in writing. Allowing children to see that their oral language can be written down and used as reading material will go a long way towards making reading a tangible and relevant activity. Many teachers are now encouraging their kindergarten students to begin writing their own stories. By doing so, the children are able to apply the knowledge learned in other areas in the language arts curriculum to immediate use.

Handwriting practice can be given as an independent exercise, or in conjunction with other reading activities. It is important to note here that equal, if not more, weight should be given to the recognition and writing of lower case letters over capital letters. This is due to the fact that, in reading books, the child must deal with lower case letters much more often than with capital letters. For most children, lower case letters are more difficult to recognize and write. Because of this, they should be introduced along with uppercase letters.

Left-right progression is an important skill that requires moving the hand from left to right in writing, or the eyes in reading. This is a skill which often does not develop naturally, but must be constantly reinforced in a variety of ways. Visual and auditory memory involve the capacity to remember what has been seen or heard and to recall that information when needed. These skills enable a child to remember letter forms, or a sequence of letter sounds which must be blended together. Visual discrimination refers to the ability to differentiate between similar letter forms, such as *b* and *d*, while auditory discrimination refers to the ability to differentiate between similar letter sounds. Visual-motor coordination involves the coordination of eye and hand movements which is essential to the writing process.

MATHEMATICS

Mathematics is a stimulating and varied subject that constitutes a great deal more than counting, adding, and subtracting. Arithmetic, as we knew it in school, involved mainly computational skills. The ability to compute easily and quickly continues to be a major focus in mathematics, but the ability to understand concepts and organize mathematical information has recently gained a deserved prominence in the curriculum.

In kindergarten, your child will learn to "count with meaning." Counting with meaning means that the child can assign a verbal or written mathematical symbol, such as 7 or *seven,* to seven actual items, be they seven fingers, seven buttons, or seven elephants. The child should be able to do this without skipping over items or counting them twice. Being able to count by rote aloud does not necessarily indicate that the child can count with meaning. Once the child has learned to count ten objects properly, she can then learn to count aloud to twenty, to one hundred, or beyond. The skill of counting with meaning is easily transferred when using numbers above ten.

Along with counting, number recognition and writing are usually taught at the beginning of the year. This is because they are skills upon which many mathematical experiences depend. Children usually learn to recognize their numbers before they are able to write them. Many of the number forms are difficult for children to make, and repeated practice in a variety of ways makes the work more pleasant. Kindergarten children should learn to write their numbers to 10, although many can move on to higher numbers.

Once children can count with meaning, as well as recognize and write their numbers, they are ready to begin working with the concepts of addition and subtraction. In the past, these concepts were taught separately. This emphasis on separating the two operations has only served to confuse children and prolong misunderstandings. Subtraction is merely the taking apart of something which you put together during addition. Today, addition and subtraction are usually taught at the same time. Children of kindergarten age will find it difficult to reverse their thinking, to think backwards, so to speak; therefore, it is important to provide them with opportunities to reverse the operation of addition as much as possible in order to develop this ability. This is most easily done with real-life materials which the children can handle and with which they are familiar, such as buttons, silverware, and toys. It is important to keep in mind that mathematics is a language, and that this language represents real-life problems. Well before kindergarten, children are familiar with situations such as, "I have six pieces of candy and I have to share them with my brother." It is beneficial to capitalize on these experiences so as to help make math a relevant part of your child's everyday life.

Another important counting skill that children should learn as they begin to work with addition and subtraction, is the skill of "counting on." When children add three apples and two oranges, they should not count the total by saying, "one, two, three (apples), four, five (oranges)." Your child should point to the three apples and say, "three" (then point to the oranges), "four, five." This skill should be reinforced each time your child does an addition activity.

In kindergarten the children are given a variety of experiences involving the manipulation of groups of objects (sets). Many kindergarten programs go on to teach the mathematical symbols of addition and subtraction ($+$, $-$, $=$). Children can also begin working with simple problems using numbers up to seven.

Other mathematical concepts covered in kindergarten include patterns, comparisons, shapes, sorting and classifying, weighing and measuring, graphing, and estimation. Working with patterns, strange as it may seem, is an excellent tool for helping children to more fully understand the number system. Once children learn to recognize and reproduce patterns of objects or sounds, they will carry this skill over to numbers, where they become attuned to looking for patterns in the number system. As an example, see how many patterns you can find in this matrix:

1	2	3	4	5	6	7	8	9	10
11	12	13	14	15	16	17	18	19	20
21	22	23	24	25	26	27	28	29	30
31	32	33	34	35	36	37	38	39	40
41	42	43	44	45	46	47	48	49	50
51	52	53	54	55	56	57	58	59	60
61	62	63	64	65	66	67	68	69	70
71	72	73	74	75	76	77	78	79	80
81	82	83	84	85	86	87	88	89	90
91	92	93	94	95	96	97	98	99	100

You may have found patterns in this matrix according to which numbers increase by 5's, 10's or 2's. This is the fundamental concept covered in multiplication. Learning to recognize patterns or systems is a fundamental way to approach learning of all kinds. The beauty of math lies in the patterns made by the numbers and their combinations.

When working with comparisons, children deal with the concepts of more and less, larger and smaller, longer and shorter, etc. These concepts should first be applied to real objects. For example, at snack time, Johnny may note that he has fewer crackers than Susie. Once children are able to identify these attributes, they can apply them to numbers, thus understanding that three crackers is less than four.

Weighing and measuring are skills which depend upon comparisons. Once a child learns to compare two objects, she can then measure them, using a standard which tells her how much of each she has and what the difference is between them. Thus, Patty is not just taller than Leah, but she is one hand, three blocks, or five inches taller. Weighing and measuring are usually done with non-standard units, such as hands, cubes, or pieces of yarn, rather than inches, meters, or pounds—concepts usually too abstract for kindergarten children.

Shape recognition is an elementary geometry skill which is often begun in preschool. In kindergarten, children usually learn to recognize circles, triangles, squares, and rectangles. Other shapes such as hexagons, diamonds, and ovals can also be introduced.

Sorting and classifying provide a means for children to order and organize their world. For the very young child, a dog may belong to only one class of objects, such as animals. As the child grows older, he learns that dogs can belong to the class of pets, of living things, mammals, things that move, or things that make noise. Thus a dog can belong to many different sets at the same time. Manipulation of these concepts encourages flexible and multi-layered thinking—the beginning of reasoning and logic.

Graphing is introduced as a method of organizing mathematical information in a pictorial mode. For example, the class could make up a graph that shows how the children come to school. The results might look like this:

Graphing is used as another means of working with counting and comparisons. Learning to read pictorial graphs is a skill that can be introduced effectively in kindergarten, although it is not usually taught in a formal manner until second or third grade.

Estimation is a math activity that provides a wide variety of benefits. When children are asked to estimate a given quantity, they must understand how to make and check their predictions. This requires complex problem-solving capabilities that utilize their understanding of the standard to be estimated, such as number, length, or weight. Repetition of estimation activities helps children toward a clear understanding of counting, number relationships, and measurement. It also helps children to connect abstract numbers to objects in the real world.

Time, as told with the calendar and the clock, is an important skill that is first introduced in kindergarten. Usually, the days of the week and months of the year are discussed, and holidays are celebrated in their various seasons. Telling time on a clock is usually limited to recognizing the hour, and sometimes the half hour.

SOCIAL STUDIES/SCIENCE/HEALTH

Social studies, science, and health studies in the kindergarten usually take their themes from the child's everyday environment. Subjects covered often include the community, transportation, the seasons, self-awareness, the five senses, holidays, nutrition, and dental health. Other subjects that often intrigue kindergarten children are dinosaurs, the sea, the circus, and plants and animals. While studying these subjects, the teacher usually provides the class with a variety of activities based on the subject matter. For example, in studying the sea, the class might 1) listen to stories; 2) paint sea animals or a mural; 3) taste salt water; 4) write stories; 5) classify sea animals; 6) collect shells; 7) visit the beach or aquarium. By providing a wide range of experiences, the teacher is presenting and reinforcing the main concepts of the unit in a realistic and developmentally sound manner. Social studies and science are wonderful subjects for stimulating interests, creative thinking, and problem-solving. Integrating math and reading skills into the unit's activities helps the child to see the interrelationships among various subjects.

ART/MUSIC/DRAMA

Kindergarten-age children often have had a great deal of experience using art materials even before entering school. This experience usually involves an investigation of the properties of the media which they are using. Most children, by the age of five, have also developed personal symbols for such common items in their drawings as houses, people, and animals. In kindergarten, children will continue to explore the properties of such materials as crayons, clay, tempra and water color paints, and collage materials. The children will also be encouraged to develop some rudimentary techniques in the use of these materials, and to pay closer attention to their use of design, shape, color, and texture.

The music curriculum in kindergarten focuses on singing and rhythm activities. The children learn a variety of songs, and can accompany these songs with clapping and body movements. Rhythm instruments, such as drums, maracas, and tambourines are used to help the children find the beat. Kindergarten children may also learn to recognize a few written notes and hand signals.

Children invoke drama, or play acting, in almost everything they do. Dramatic play occurs spontaneously when children play with dolls or puppets, build with blocks, or play dress-up. In this type of play, children are initiating and trying out social roles that they observe at home, on television, and in the community. In addition to providing opportunities for spontaneous dramatic play, the kindergarten teacher will engage the children in more formal dramatic activities such as puppet shows and plays.

7

PHYSICAL EDUCATION

Formal physical education programs are often neglected for younger children on the premise that the children get enough exercise naturally. However, it has been found that children, like adults, need regular strenuous exercise. Physical education programs in kindergarten usually focus on individual movement and rhythm exploration. Such activities include the use of a variety of equipment, such as balls, climbing equipment, jump ropes, and bean bags. Children are encouraged to draw upon an ever-increasing understanding of their bodies in order to refine such movements as running, skipping, climbing, hopping, and jumping. Some loosely organized games may be introduced, so that children begin to use these skills in a group context. Highly structured games, such as kickball, are inappropriate for this age group. Rhythm and dance movements are additional, highly enjoyable ways to explore movement possibilities and to gain body control and self-confidence.

SOCIAL DEVELOPMENT

Kindergarten is an important year for learning social skills. The focus for children is on developing an ability to accept differences, share people and resources, cooperate on group projects, and participate in group discussions. Sharing friends or equipment can be difficult for kindergarten children. Providing for a system of fair distribution—one that includes delayed gratification—helps the child to see that his needs are being considered, even if they will not always be met immediately. As kindergarten children begin to develop longer-lasting peer relationships, they become more aware of the responsibilities inherent in maintaining those relationships. Giving children socially positive and acceptable ways to solve their differences with others goes a long way toward helping them gain independence. Class discussions concerning social problems and ways to solve them are very helpful for modeling appropriate techniques. During this year, young children are also expected to learn proper classroom behavior. This might include: self-control, working independently, time management, and neatness. Class helpers are often utilized to help the children learn to handle and enjoy responsibilities.

Chapter Two: **Spending Time with Your Child— Tips and Techniques**

Educators have come to recognize the important role that parents play as the primary educators of their children. The issue is not whether a parent should teach his child, but how. Perhaps the most important point that can be made concerns the time that you spend with your child. The most educationally productive times occur more often during spontaneous and informal exchanges. Learning is too often viewed as an adult-dominated activity, i.e. the teacher gives the knowledge and the child receives it. We have come to understand that learning is an interactive process that takes place between the child and his environment. Many situations can be turned into learning experiences by taking cues from your child's interests and questions and expanding upon them. The advantage to using informal situations to broaden your child's knowledge is that you are capitalizing on an interest that is already there. Learning to take a question, such as "What's for dinner?" or an observation such as "That truck is very noisy!" and turn it into a learning experience is a skill that will increase with practice. Here are some tips that may help speed this along:

1) Talk *with* your children rather than *at* them. Use new and descriptive words so as to enrich your child's vocabulary.

2) Ask questions that are thought-provoking and require more than one-word answers. Many teachers use a technique called "wait time." This involves waiting for the child's answer for five, ten, or even twenty seconds. By doing so, you are encouraging your child to rely on herself to think through the answer.

3) Listen to your children. Encourage them to talk, speculate, and ask questions. Make sure that you give them the chance to initiate conversations. Children will seek to express themselves if they know you will give them your attention.

4) Praise your children, not only for giving the "right" answer, but for asking questions that show an interest.

These same techniques should be used when working with your child in a more formal situation, such as teaching her to write her name or finding pictures in a magazine of things that start with the letter *t*. Here are some additional suggestions that may help to make your lessons more enjoyable and productive.

1) Be patient. Trying to teach your child a specific skill may become a frustrating experience. During the lessons, your child may make the same mistake many times. It is important that you don't become angry or impatient, since learning cannot take place in a tense atmosphere. If you find yourself tense, drop the lesson and do something else for a while.

2) Constantly reevaluate your expectations and your child's progress. If your child isn't achieving the goal you have set for her, she may not be ready for, or interested in the activity. If you feel that this is the case, you should postpone the lessons until your child indicates an interest.

3) Frequent, short lessons are more effective than long intermittent ones. With short lessons, your child may be able to pay full attention and have frequent opportunities to practice. Fifteen minutes to half an hour is a reasonable time to expect a five-year-old to pay attention. Scheduling your lessons at a regular time may also be helpful, and it will set the stage for good study habits later on.

4) Once your child has mastered a certain skill, he will wish to use and refine it. For example, once your child has learned to write his name, he may wish to use his new-found ability to label his clothes and toys. After writing his first name becomes old hat, he may wish to learn to write his last name.

5) Above all, make the lessons as enjoyable as possible. Your child will look forward to the time you spend together as well as to learning new skills.

A short note on paying attention. A common remark heard at conference time is that Johnny has trouble paying attention. Admittedly, it's very hard for Johnny to listen to the teacher when poking Susie (chewing an eraser, digging a hole in his desk) provides so much more entertainment. As adults, we may do the same sorts of things during a dull lecture, but we learn to make our distractions less noticeable to others. It would be best if we were interested in the lecture, but that cannot always be the case. We have learned to control our behavior and focus our attention on the task at hand. As teachers of children, we all can help them pay attention by:

1) Making sure that the activity is appropriate and interesting.

2) Providing for the child's innate desire to move and manipulate things.

3) Removing unnecessary distractions and temptations. Anticipating your child's difficulties as well as interests will make your time together more pleasurable.

Chapter Three: **Activities**

LANGUAGE ARTS

READING TO YOUR CHILD

Because reading to your child is such a valuable exercise, I would like to say a few short words before we get down to specific activities. I have yet to meet a child who is not delighted to be read to by a parent, but it is important to read *with* your child, not only to her. When your child interrupts a story, it is because she is curious, interested, or intrigued. Very often children relate what they see in a book to something they are already familiar with. A young child may see the wolf in *Little Red Riding Hood* and comment that it looks like a dog. Thus this child is making a connection between new and familiar material—the essence of the learning process. These interruptions can be used as cues to further a child's knowledge. A follow-up activity for this child would be to take out a book on wolves from the library, or visit the zoo to see a wolf. Stories that contain familiar characters or characters relevant to young children, such as fairy tales, are important aids for personal and moral development. Children easily identify with characters in enjoyable stories. When these characters solve problems within the story, children will take the cues to help them find solutions in their own lives. When children are regularly exposed to material of good literary quality, listening and speaking vocabularies, as well as general knowledge, are also enriched. This equips the child himself to be a more meaningful reader.

1. Story Time

Concepts: Language Enrichment, Creative Thinking, Literature Appreciation, Plot and Character Development

Purpose: To use language and thinking in stories

Situation: Leisure time

Materials: Storybook

Activity: After reading a story, ask your child one of the following questions. Listen to your child's response and discuss what led him to give the answer he did.

1) Can you make up a different ending to the story?
2) Can you think of another person or animal who could be in this story? How would the story be different?
3) Can you think of a different place this story could have happened? Would the story be different if it happened in a forest, cave, city, etc.?
4) What would have happened if . . . (the woodsman didn't save Red Riding Hood, Snow White didn't eat the poisoned apple, etc.)?
5) Can you pretend that you're the author and keep the story going?
6) Would you feel the way so-and-so did if such-and-such happened to you?
7) Has anything like this ever happened to you?
8) What would it be like if this (animals could talk, magic was real, etc.) would really happen?

2. Finish the Story

Concepts: Language Enrichment, Creative
Thinking, Plot and Character
Development, Sequencing
Purpose: To tell a coherent story
Situation: Traveling in the car, leisure time
Materials: None

Activity: Give your child an opening
sentence, such as "Once upon a time, there
was a pirate ship . . . ." Let your child tell the
story from there. Encourage a coherent plot
line and a definite ending.

Variation I: Make it a family activity by
taking turns adding just one idea at a time
until the story is complete.

Variation II: Using the same format, let your
child tell a story from a picture, such as a
newspaper or magazine picture.

Variation III: Let your child make up the
story to a wordless picture book, such as
Rain by Peter Spier. Ask your librarian for a
list of such books.

Variation IV: Hand your child an object such
as a seashell. Have him tell a story about it,
such as "One day, a seashell was lying on a
beach. A little boy picked it up and put it in
his pocket . . . ."

3. Short Stories

Concepts: Sequencing, Language
Enrichment
Purpose: To put pictures in order so that
they tell a story
Situation: Leisure time
Materials: Old magazines, scissors, paper,
stapler, pencil

Activity: In this activity, your child should
look through magazines to find three or four
pictures that would tell a story when put
together. (You may need to give some help
in this stage of the activity.) Cut the pictures
out and staple them, in order, on a sheet of
paper. Your child can dictate a story to go
with the pictures.

Variation: Staple together three single
pictures cut from old magazines, such as a
picture of a house, an elephant, and a ball.
Let your child make up a sentence that
includes all the items, such as "The elephant
played ball in his house." The sillier the
sentence, the better. (If your child can read,
he can write the sentence himself.) You can
also pick one or two words from the
sentence and write them on index cards.
Use these words to add to your child's sight-
word vocabulary.

4. Guessing Games

Concepts: Language Enrichment, Logical
Thinking, Classification
Purpose: To guess what an object is by
asking questions about it
Situation: Traveling in the car, leisure time
Materials: A collection of small objects,
such as toys or kitchen items

Activity: Choose one of the items and hide
it behind your back. Your child must try to
guess the item's identity by asking questions
that can only be answered with *yes* or *no*. (It
may take a couple of sessions before your
child learns to ask questions to gain
information about the object, rather than
taking guesses immediately.) If after ten
questions, the identity of the item is not
discovered, show your child the object and
pick a new one to identify. When your child
guesses correctly, she may take a turn being
the leader.

Variation I: Using a collection of small
objects, play a game called What Is It? Tell
your child that you are thinking of an animal,
food, toy, etc. Describe the object giving at
least two clues. (It is brown, furry, and you
can sleep with it. What is it? A teddy bear!) If
your child guesses the correct answer, let
her be the leader.

Variation II: For a more difficult variation,
play the old 20 Questions game. Think of an
item and have your child guess it by asking
yes or *no* questions to gain information.

5. Finger Games

Concept: Rhyming Words
Purpose: To fill in a rhyming word
Situation: Leisure time
Materials: None

Teach your child these rhyming finger games. Once your child has heard the words, do not say the final rhyme word. Let him fill it in.

Open, shut them .... (open and close both hands)
Open, shut them.
Give your hands a clap.. (clap your hands)
Open, shut them .... (open and close both hands)
Open, shut them.
Lay them in your lap.. (fold hands in lap)
Creep them, creep them .... (creep fingers up your neck)
Creep them, creep them .... (creep fingers up your chin)
Right up to your chin.
Open up your little mouth .... (open your mouth)
But do not let them *in*!

Ten little Martians .... (hold up 10 fingers)
Standing in a row.
When they see the captain,
They bow just so .... (bend your fingers up and down)
They march to the left........................... (move both hands with a marching
and they march to the right.   rhythm to left and right.)
Then they close their eyes........................... (palms together under the side
And they sleep all *night*.   of the face as if sleeping)

Five little monkeys .... (hold up five fingers and
Jumping on the bed.   move up and down as if jumping)
One fell off and
bumped his head... (hold head as if hurt)
Mama called the doctor and............................... (pretend you are making a
the doctor said,   telephone call)
"No more monkeys
Jumping on the *bed*!".................................. (wag finger in admonishment)
(Repeat verse with four, three, etc.

                13

6. Short Poems

Concept: Rhyming Words
Purpose: To fill in a rhyming word
Situation: Traveling in the car
Materials: None

Activity: Make up a short, two-line poem, but leave out the final rhyming word. (We drive in our car. It travels very ___.) Ask your child to finish the poem. Then let him make up his own. This is a good rhyming activity for children who are just beginning to get the idea of rhyme.

7. Rhyme Time

Concept: Rhyming Words
Purpose: To think of a word that rhymes with an object you see
Situation: Traveling in the car
Materials: None

Activity: Before playing this game, make sure that your child is beginning to understand the concept of rhyme. Read her stories and poems that rhyme (Dr. Seuss books and Mother Goose nursery rhymes are great). Your child should be able to tell you when two words rhyme before playing this game.

As you are driving in the car, have your child start off the game by saying the name of something she sees out the window, such as *tree* or *car*. You respond by saying a word that rhymes with the object your child saw. Now it is your turn to give a word and have your child think of its rhyme. If she can't think of a word that rhymes, you may go again, and vice versa.

Variations: Try to think of as many words as you can that rhyme with the first word before giving up your turn. See who can think of the longest word to rhyme with the first. How about the shortest?

8. Robot

Concepts: Direction Words, Descriptive Vocabulary, Logical Thinking
Purpose: To understand direction words such as *up*, *down*, *right*, and *left*
Situation: Leisure time
Materials: None

Activity: This game, in addition to helping children understand direction words, encourages them to see things from a different point of view. This type of activity is used in a variety of forms in many classrooms to help children understand how a computer works. To begin this game, have the adult be the robot first. Your child must give you *specific*, verbal directions (no pointing!) for tying your shoe (or opening a window, making a peanut butter and jelly sandwich, etc.). Your child must give the directions using the proper vocabulary, and in the proper order. It is not easy! This game can also be played with two children, one playing the robot and one giving the directions.

Variation: Make a simple design or pattern out of dominoes, tinker toys, blocks, etc. Hiding the design, and with your back to the child, give her the exact directions necessary to complete the design. When your child completes her design, compare the designs. Then switch places, letting your child make the model and give you directions for building it.

LETTER RECOGNITION

The following activities are designed to teach the names and the sounds of the letters. You should emphasize that letters have both a name and a sound. When your child can listen to the word *snake* and tell you that the sound at the beginning of the word is "sss," then he is ready to connect the sound with the written letter. Until then, working with your child on letter recognition will help your child become familiar with the forms of the letters. If your child shows early readiness to learn the letter sounds, then you can combine the two concepts. When working with letter names and letter sounds, make sure that you use both lower and upper case forms! Many of the activities involve matching the upper and lower case forms of a letter. It is not necessary to teach the letter names in the order of the alphabet. It will probably be more meaningful to your child if you start with the letters of his name. Being able to form the letters is an equally important skill, so be sure to include handwriting practice as part of your activities.

When working with letter sounds, there are two pitfalls to avoid. The first is to avoid the blanket statement *B* is for *ball*. *B* is only for *ball* when you have made the connection between the letter name *B* and the sound "B." Memorizing a key word for each letter will do no good until the child can hear and identify the sound at the beginning of the word. The other pitfall to avoid is that of adding a vowel sound after the consonant sound. The sound of the letter *T* is not "tee" but "t." Do not inadvertently add an extra vowel sound to the consonants, or your child will have difficulty when the time comes to blend the sounds together into a word. Begin with the consonants whose sounds are much like their names, such as *s, m* and *f*. You may wish to introduce the letter sounds in this order: *m, s, f, t, r, h, l, a,* (as in *apple*), *n, p, d, i* (as in *inch*), *b, g,* (as in *girl*), *c* (as in *cat*), *v, o* (as in *pot*), *k, j, w, y, z, e* (as in *pet*), and *u* (as in *umbrella*). (However, keep in mind that kindergarten teachers introduce the letter sounds in a variety of sequences and ways. To be consistent, you may want to consult your child's teacher before covering the letter sounds.) The first few letter sounds may be difficult for your child, but once he grasps the concept, the rest will come easily.

9. The Alphabet Song

Concept: Letter Name Recognition
Purpose: To say the alphabet in order
Situation: Traveling in the car, leisure time
Materials: None

Activity: Learning to say the alphabet is not absolutely essential to beginning reading, but it does not hurt. The easiest way to learn to recite the alphabet is that old standby, the Alphabet Song. Make sure as you sing the song, that you articulate the verse "L, M, N, O, P" clearly. Many children have the impression that it is all one sound. Once your child has learned to sing the song, work on reciting the alphabet without the music. It will help your child's letter recognition skills if you have a copy of the alphabet in front of you as you sing, pointing to each letter as you go along.

10. Alphabet Books

Concept: Letter Name Recognition
Purpose: To recognize and name upper and lower case letters
Situation: Leisure time
Materials: Alphabet book(s) in which the letters (both upper and lower case on the same page) are large and clear, with perhaps one or two pictures

Activity: Looking at alphabet books can be done in the same way as you read other books with your child. As you look through the book, you might say, "See, this is an *A*. It comes to a point at the top and has a bar across the middle. Can you say 'A'? This is the capital *A*, and this is the lower case *a*. Do you have an *A* in your name?" You may have your child trace the letter with her finger, using the proper strokes. You can also look through other books to locate both an upper and lower case *A*.

If your child makes a mistake and calls an *H* by the name of "A," don't be discouraged. You may remind her of the difference by saying, "Well, that does have a bar across the middle, but remember, 'A' has a point at the top." Some letters, such as *b*, *d*, and *p* will be hard to distinguish because of similar formations. Many children do not learn to differentiate between them until as late as second grade, so do not be concerned. To help your child to differentiate between lower case *b* and *d*, try this old teacher trick. With your right hand, make a circle with your thumb and forefinger. Extend the rest of your fingers upright. (You have made a lower case *d*.) Now do the same with your left hand. (Now you have made a *b*.) Place them together with the circles touching and the rest of your fingers upright. It looks like a bed! The *b* is the head of the bed, the *d* the foot. It also looks like the written word bed.

11. Looking for Letters

Concepts: Letter Name Recognition, Visual Discrimination
Purpose: To learn the names of upper and lower case letter forms, and to put the letters in alphabetical order
Situation: Leisure time
Materials: Set of twenty-six index cards, with the upper case letter forms written on one side, and the lower case forms on the other

Activity: Lay the cards out in alphabetical order on a table. Tell your child that you want her to have collected all the letters by the end of the game. Name each letter, out of order, describing some of the letter's characteristics ("Mary, I'm going to name a letter. Find that letter and take it. Find the *M*. Remember, the *M* is the first letter in your name. It looks like two mountains standing together.") Have your child find the letter and hold onto it. When all the letters have been taken, reverse the process by naming the letters in alphabetical order. Your child should locate the letter in her pile and place it back on the table. Do this first with all upper case letters, then with all lower case letters.

Variation: This is an excellent activity to use if you have magnetic letters. Try playing the same game, but call for letters that spell a message ("Hi Dad") and leave it on the refrigerator!

12. Matching Letters

Concept: Letter Name Recognition
Purpose: To match the lower case letter forms with the upper case forms
Situation: Leisure time
Materials: Set of index cards in random order, with the lower and upper case forms written singly on each one. Your child can help make the cards by writing the letters herself.

Activity: Play a modified game of Fish. Deal 8 cards to each person. The players, in turn, ask one another if they have the match to one of their cards. If the player who was asked has the card, he must turn it over. If he does not, he says "Go fish." The player who asked for the card must take another from the deck. The pairs are collected, and the person with the most pairs when all the cards are played out is the winner.

13. Guess the Letter

Concepts: Letter Name Recognition, Alphabetical Order
Purpose: To understand alphabetical order
Situation: Leisure time, traveling in the car
Materials: Copy of the alphabet

Activity: When you play this game initially, have a copy of the alphabet around as a reference. Tell your child that you're going to play a game to see if she can tell the letter that you're thinking of. Proceed by asking such questions as: "I'm thinking of the first letter of the alphabet. Can you guess it?" "I'm thinking of the letter that comes after *J*." "I'm thinking of the letter that comes before *S*." "I'm thinking of the letter that comes between *T* and *V*." When your child becomes more familiar with the alphabet, try this activity without the written letters in front of her.

Variation: This activity works equally well with numbers ("I'm thinking of the number that comes before 13. Can you guess it?" "I'm thinking of the number that comes after 99.")

14. Cornmeal Letters

Concepts: Letter Name Recognition, Letter Writing, Spelling
Purpose: To write the letters of the alphabet
Situation: Working in the kitchen, leisure time
Materials: yellow cornmeal—about $\frac{3}{4}$ cups, cookie sheet with sides

Activity: Pour the cornmeal onto the cookie sheet. Working on a few letters at a time, (perhaps starting with the letters in your child's name), practice writing with the index finger. This activity has several benefits. The child can write many, many letters or numbers without using up reams of paper. If a mistake is made, it is easily erased. This activity also provides the child with plenty of tactile input, which helps her remember the stroke sequence. If your child is reading, have her spell simple sight or phonetic words instead of writing individual letters. This activity works equally well with number writing.

Variation: Salt or sand can be used in place of the cornmeal. For a delicious activity, mix up a batch of chocolate pudding and plop a spoonful on a large plate or waterproof table. After practicing his letters, your child can eat the results! Shaving cream can also be used in this manner or directly on a table top. It is not edible, but it smells good and cleans your table beautifully.

15. Pretzel Letters

Concepts: Letter Name Recognition, Letter Writing, Spelling
Purpose: To form letters using pretzel sticks
Situation: Working in the kitchen, leisure time
Materials: Bag of pretzel sticks

Activity: With a copy of the alphabet handy, have your child form letters using the pretzel sticks. To make rounded letters, break the sticks into smaller pieces. You can also form numbers and spell words—the possibilities are endlessly delicious!

16. Rainbow Letters

Concepts: Letter Name Recognition, Letter Writing
Purpose: To practice handwriting
Situation: Leisure time
Materials: Crayons, pencil, writing paper

Activity: Have your child practice letters with pencil first, then make "rainbows" by tracing over each letter with different colored crayons. This activity lends itself well to sign and poster making. This activity can also be done with numbers.

17. Backtracing

Concepts: Letter Name Recognition, Letter Writing
Purpose: To recognize letters
Situation: Traveling in the car, leisure time
Materials: None

Activity: To begin this game, tell your child that you will be tracing some letters on her back and you want her to guess what they are. If your child is just learning the alphabet, tell her the letters that you will be working with beforehand so that she may form a mental picture of them. It will also help initially to have a copy of the alphabet handy for her to refer to. Once she has guessed the letters (do both lower and upper case) that you have traced on her back, let her write some on your back. Your child will be gaining important tactical feedback, and you will easily be able to tell if she has formed the letters using the proper stroke sequence. You may also wish to practice number writing or spelling with this activity.

18. Grocery List

Concepts: Letter Writing, Letter Sounds, Spelling
Purpose: To practice handwriting
Situation: Working in the kitchen
Materials: Paper and pencil

Activity: Dictate your grocery list to your child, one letter at a time. If your child has mastered the letter sounds, say the name of the item and let him spell the word himself by sounding it out. At the market, your child can then read the list back to you as you shop. (P.S., this activity takes plenty of time!)

19. Letter Pictures

Concepts: Letter Name Recognition, Letter Writing
Purpose: To turn a letter form into a picture
Situation: Leisure time
Materials: Crayons, paper

Activity: Ask your child to draw a letter that he has been working on. Then have him turn the paper around and around, looking at the letter from every angle, trying to visualize an animal or object suggested by the lines. Using the letter form as a basis for a picture, draw around, not on the letter. Let the other members of the family guess which letter is contained in the picture. This activity can also be done with numbers.

20. Letter Search

Concepts: Letter Name Recognition, Letter Sounds
Purpose: To find familiar letters
Situation: Shopping, traveling in the car
Materials: None

Activity: This activity merely involves taking advantage of the words that surround your child in her daily life. Choose one or two letter names or letter sounds that you will look for on your trip. As you're riding in the car or shopping in the supermarket, see how many times you can find and identify the letter, or an object whose name begins with the letter sound you are looking for. License plates, traffic signs, billboards, and store signs can all help you in your search.

Variation: As you listen to the radio, television, or records, have your child clap or raise her hand each time she hears the letter sound you have picked to work on.

21. Letter Bags

Concept: Letter Sounds
Purpose: To collect household items that begin with the same letter sounds
Situation: Leisure time
Materials: Several large grocery bags

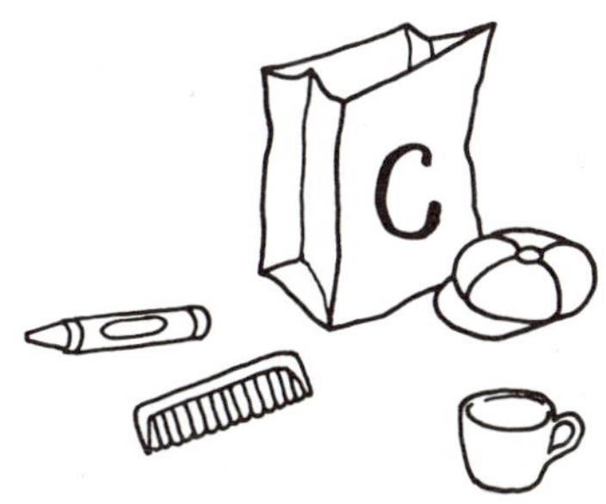

Activity: Choose several letter sounds to work with, then print one letter on each bag. Have your child see how many items she can find around the house that begin with those sounds, and have her put them in the bags.

Variation: For a birthday party, turn this activity into a treasure hunt. The child (or pair or group) that has the most "treasures" in their bag is the winner!

22. Begins Like . . . .

Concepts: Letter Sounds, Auditory Discrimination
Purpose: To think of a word that begins with the same sound as another word
Situation: Traveling in the car
Materials: None

Activity: Tell your child that you are going to say a word, such as *table.* (Say the word, and the sound of the beginning letter, "t.") Ask your child to say the word and the sound several times. Now ask your child if she can think of another word that begins with the same sound as *table.* Continue this way, using a variety of sounds. This activity helps to train your child to listen for beginning sounds. No knowledge of letters is even necessary.

23. I Spy

Concepts: Letter Sounds, Auditory Discrimination
Purpose: To find an object that begins with the same sound as a given word
Situation: Leisure time, traveling in the car, outside
Materials: None

Activity: Say, "I spy with my little eye, something in the room (park, car, etc.) that begins with the sound "s." Can you guess what I see?" *Sun, soap,* or *seat* would be appropriate answers.

24. Sound Collage

Concept: Letter Sounds
Purpose: To find pictures of objects whose names begin with a certain letter sound
Situation: Leisure time
Materials: Old magazines, glue, scissors, paper

Activity: Choose a letter sound to work on. Have your child look through old magazines, cutting out pictures of objects that begin with that sound. Your child may need help with this activity for the first few sessions. A helpful hint: have him name all the objects pictured on each page, and listen for the sound at the beginning of each word he says. Glue the cut-out pictures onto the paper.

25. ABC Dusting

Concept: Letter Sounds
Purpose: To locate objects within the house that begin with a certain letter sound
Situation: Cleaning the house
Materials: Dust rag

Activity: Begin with the letter sounds with which your child is most familiar. Working on one letter sound at a time, such as "t", dust all the objects in the house that begin with "t", such as *table*, *toys*, and *television*. When you finish with "t", continue with other letter sounds until your whole house is clean!

26. Sound Stories

Concept: Letter Sounds
Purpose: To put together a short story using as many words that begin with the same sound as possible
Situation: Traveling in the car
Materials: None

Activity: The object of this activity is to make up silly stories of perhaps one, two, or three sentences, using as many words that begin with the same sound as you can think of. Make this a joint venture between you or an older sibling and your child. An example would be, "One day, I saw a silly spotted snake named Sam. Sam spied me, and slithered over to say, "Hi Sally!"

NAME WRITING

For a kindergarten child, being able to print his own name is a big accomplishment. For the kindergarten teacher, it is a wonderful time-saver. Imagine the time it takes to put the names of 20 children on two work papers a day, not to mention all the pictures produced by the average kindergarten class each day! Printing a name, unless it happens to be very long, should be quite easy to learn.

27. Printing Practice

Concept: Name Writing
Purpose: To print one's name by correctly forming the letters
Situation: Leisure time
Materials: Paper, pencil

Activity: As you print your child's name, have him stand next to you so that the letters are right side up. By printing the name in lower case letters and using the standard stroke sequence, your child can learn to write his name correctly the first time around. Print the name clearly and make the letters fairly big, spelling the name out as you write. After you've done this several times, ask your child if he can remember the letters in his name. Finally, let your child try his hand. Give him a large piece of paper with his name printed at the top and let him go to town! He can also practice in corn meal, salt, or sand. Check in once in a while to make sure that he is forming the letters properly.

LEFT-TO-RIGHT PROGRESSION

Left to right progression involves training the eyes and hands to move from left to right when reading and writing. This skill is most easily developed on an informal basis. As you read a story book or the Sunday comics, occasionally move your hand across the page and point out that you always start at the left side and move across to the right. If your child enjoys practicing his name or letters but has trouble remembering which side of the paper to start on, put a green dot on the left side (for "go") and a red dot on the right side (for "stop"). The following activities may also help to reinforce this concept.

28. Sunday Comics

Concepts: Left-to-Right Progression, Sequencing
Purpose: To put the pictures of a comic strip in order
Situation: Leisure time
Materials: Scissors, comics, glue

Activity: Choose a comic strip in which the pictures clearly show the sequence of activities. Read the comic strip together and discuss the sequence of events with your child. Let your child cut out the pictures, scramble them up and glue them back down in the correct order.

21

29. Shape Patterns

Concepts: Left-to-Right Progression,
   Shape Recognition, Patterns, Sequencing
Purpose: To complete a pattern of shapes
   that moves from left to right
Situation: Leisure time
Materials: 5 different colors of paper,
   scissors, glue

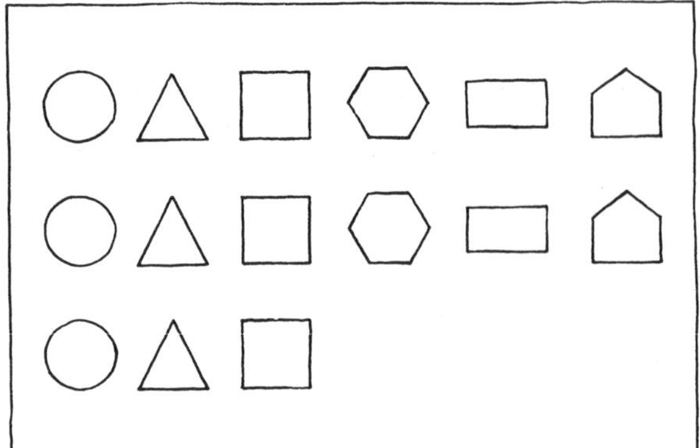

Activity: Trace several copies of five
different shapes on the colored paper. Use a
different shape for each color. Your child may
enjoy helping to cut them out. Make sure
that one of the shapes is red and one is
green. Glue the shapes in a line across the
top of the paper, starting the pattern with the
green shape and ending with the red. Have
your child continue the pattern by pasting on
the same sequence of shapes over and over
again, always beginning at the green shape
and stopping at the red. Continue until the
paper is filled up. When it is dry, it can be
sprayed with a clear lacquer or covered with
clear contact paper and used as a pretty
placemat.

Variation: This same concept can be
transferred to peg board designs if your child
has a set. Start a pattern with a green peg
on the left and complete it with a red peg on
the far right.

30. Do You Remember?

Concept: Visual Memory
Purpose: To remember objects in a set
   after they have been taken away
Situation: Leisure time
Materials: Set of 3 or more objects, cookie
   sheet or tray

Activity: Place three different objects on
the tray. Have your child look at them very
carefully, then remove them. Ask your child
to name the three objects. Bring the tray
back and let her see how well she did. If she
does well recalling three toys, increase the
number to four or five.

Variation I: This same activity can be done
with animal crackers. Put several different
crackers on a table. Let your child study
them, then cover them up. If your child can
name all the animals that are hiding, she can
eat them.

Variation II: Place a small number of toys or
other objects on a table. Have your child
close her eyes while you remove one thing
and hide it behind your back. Then ask her
to open her eyes and tell you which toy is
missing.

31. Find the Page

Concept: Visual Memory
Purpose: To find a page in a book after
   having looked at it once
Situation: Leisure time
Materials: Picture book

Activity: Open the picture book to any
page. Have your child look at it for a minute.
Close the book. Then ask your child to find
that same page. It may help him if you
describe aloud what is in the picture before
the book is closed.

Variation: Find a picture in a book that has
many objects in it. Have your child study the
picture for several minutes, then close the
book. See how many things she can
remember that are in the picture.

32. Concentration

Concepts: Visual Memory, Visual Discrimination, Sight Word Vocabulary
Purpose: To remember where a card is placed once it has been turned over
Situation: Leisure time
Materials: Deck of playing cards

Activity: Take out five pairs of cards, such as the eight of spades and eight of clubs. Place them, face down, out of order, on a table. The first player turns over two cards, hoping to find a matching pair. If he does, he keeps the pair. If he doesn't, he must turn the cards face down again and the next player takes a turn. When all the cards have been played out, the player with the most pairs is the winner. When your child has no difficulty with five pairs, increase the number. A commercial variation of this game is available in most toy stores.

Variation: You will need some 3 $\times$ 5 index cards for this activity. Print the names of classmates or members of the family on the index cards. Start with about seven names, writing each name on two cards so that you have a pair. Play this game as you would Concentration. Beginning reading vocabulary can be substituted for names on the index cards.

33. My Shadow

Concept: Visual Memory
Purpose: To copy the actions of an adult
Situation: Leisure time
Materials: None

Activity: Do a movement, such as jumping once, and have your child imitate you. Then do the first movement (jump) and add a second (turn around). Keep adding movements, always performing them in sequence and allowing your child to imitate you each time. How many can you remember?

34. Telephone

Concept: Auditory Memory
Purpose: To remember and repeat a message
Situation: Leisure time, children's birthday or slumber party
Materials: None

Activity: You will need at least five players for this game. Sit in a circle. One player starts off the game by whispering a message—from two to six words long—to the person on her left. That person passes the message on to the next player, and so on to the last person, who has to say the message aloud. Compare the last message with the original one. The closer you have come to the original message, the better you've done.

35. I'm Going on a Trip

Concept: Auditory Memory
Purpose: To remember a series of objects
Situation: Leisure time, children's birthday party
Materials: None

Activity: You will need at least six players for this game. Sitting in a circle, one player begins the game by saying, "I'm going on a trip, and in my suitcase I've packed . . ." He then fills in that space with an item, such as an umbrella. The next player says, "I'm going on a trip, and in my suitcase I've packed an umbrella and a . . . ," filling in the space with another item. Each player must name what has been packed before, adding a new item. If he forgets an item, he is out. The game continues until there is only one person left.

36. Silly Simon Says

Concepts: Auditory Memory, Direction
  Words
Purpose: To remember a series of
  directions in order
Situation: Leisure time, children's birthday
  party
Materials: None

Activity: This game can be played with an
adult or an older sibling. Begin by giving your
child a series of two or three silly directions.
Such as, "Simon says walk backwards to the
window, put your nose on the window pane,
and scratch your ear." Make sure your child
does the actions in the proper sequence.
Keep adding additional directions as your
child improves.

37. TV Reporter

Concepts: Auditory Memory, Descriptive
  Vocabulary, Sequencing
Purpose: To accurately describe a
  television show
Situation: Leisure time
Materials: None

Activity: Pick out a television show that you
and your child enjoy. Watch the show
together, then have your child describe what
she remembers of the show. You may
explain what a reporter does, and give your
child a pencil as a pretend microphone to
use as she gives her account. This can also
be done with theater movies or movies of
family trips.

38. Make-A-Letter

Concepts: Visual Discrimination, Letter
  Name Recognition
Purpose: To practice forming letters out of
  a variety of cut-out shapes
Situation: Leisure time
Materials: Colored construction paper,
  scissors

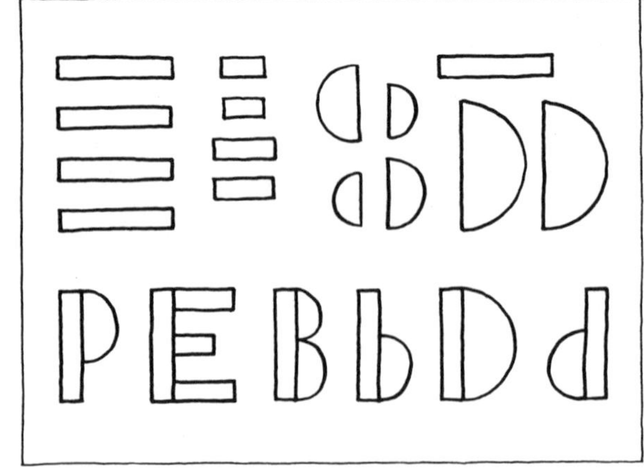

Activity: Cut a number of long and short
bars, and small and large semicircles from
colored construction paper. Show your child
how the shapes can be combined in a
variety of ways to make both upper and
lower case letters. (You may want to have a
copy of the alphabet to use as a reference).
Let your child experiment with the shapes to
create different letters. When he is done, he
can glue the letters down on paper. He might
spell out a message and create his own
birthday or Mother's Day card!

39. Circle the Word

Concepts: Visual Discrimination, Sight
  Word Vocabulary
Purpose: To find a word within a page of
  print
Situation: Leisure time
Materials: Magazines, felt-tip pen

Activity: This activity is more advanced
than many others. Ask your child's teacher
what sight words your child may be working
on at school. Common words, such as *the,
to, was,* and *he* are good to start with since
they appear frequently in any page of text.
Have your child scan a page, circling the
word whenever it appears. This activity can
be done on a more informal basis by having
your child pick out a designated word on a
story book page.

40. Lost & Found

Concepts: Visual Discrimination,
 Descriptive Vocabulary, Logical Thinking
Purpose: To accurately describe an object
Situation: Leisure time
Materials: About five pairs of shoes;
 screen, such as a blanket, thrown over a
 chair

Activity: Gather together five pairs of shoes from around the house. Take one shoe from each pair and give it to your child. Tell her to go behind the screen so that she can no longer see the other shoes. Begin the game by choosing one of the shoes and describing it aloud to your child. Do not use your hands and do not show her the shoe. Your child has three guesses to find the mate of the shoe that you have described in her pile. Have her hold up the shoe that matches your description. If she cannot find the shoe you have described, choose another and try again. When your child guesses correctly, she gets to keep the pair. Then it is her turn to choose a shoe from her pile and describe it to you. When the shoes have all been matched, the player with the most pairs is the winner.

41. What Do You Hear?

Concept: Auditory Discrimination
Purpose: To identify a variety of sounds
Situation: Almost anywhere
Materials: None

Activity: This activity merely requires that your child close her eyes and listen to the sounds around her. It can be done inside or outside, in a store or on a street corner. You can make this game more interesting by asking your child to listen for certain kinds of sounds. Try listening for sounds that are human-made versus nature-made, sounds from things that move, high and low-pitched sounds, or sounds coming from a particular direction.

42. In the Box

Concept: Auditory Discrimination
Purpose: To identify an object by the
 sound it makes
Situation: Leisure time
Materials: Several very different objects,
 such as a shoe, article of clothing, button,
 or book; cardboard box

Activity: After showing the objects to your child, place one in the box and shake it. Have your child guess which object it is by the sound it makes. You can make the game more difficult by not showing the objects to your child ahead of time.

43. Hide and Seek

Concept: Auditory Discrimination
Purpose: To find a ticking clock
Situation: Leisure time
Materials: Blindfold, wind-up clock or
 kitchen timer

Activity: Hide the clock or timer somewhere in a room. Have your child close her eyes and try to find it by listening to the ticking sound. After she finds it, have her hide the clock and you find it!

VISUAL-MOTOR COORDINATION

Some children in kindergarten will encounter difficulty with the many visual-motor activities, such as writing and drawing, that they are asked to do. For some of these children, this difficulty comes from a lack of exposure to the tasks. For others, their skills in this area will improve as they mature. However, the inability to form a recognizable letter or picture can be a very frustrating experience. Providing activities at home that help to develop this coordination without requiring a perfectly completed end product is a valuable contribution to your child's schooling and to his self-confidence.

44. Homemade Playdough

Concept: Visual-Motor Coordination
Purpose: To develop manual dexterity
Situation: In the kitchen
Materials: 2 cups white flour
  1 cup salt
  1 tablespoon alum (available in the spice section of most supermarkets)
  2 cups water
  2 tablespoons salad oil
  food coloring
1) Mix dry ingredients thoroughly.
2) Boil together water, oil, and food coloring.
3) Pour water mixture into dry ingredients and mix thoroughly.
4) Let cool until it can be handled, then knead until smooth. After dough has cooled, store in an airtight container.

Activity: The first part of the activity is, of course, making the dough with your child. The second is sitting back and letting your child enjoy himself for hours while simultaneously developing his manual dexterity. While your child works with the clay, have him try several of these movements: roll the clay into a ball; roll the clay into a sausage shape; put a ball of clay in one hand and squeeze it until the clay comes out between his fingers; make animal or people shapes by rolling the clay into balls of different sizes and pressing them together. Encourage your child to try using additional implements, such as pencils, knives, or rolling pins to add definition to his figures.

45. Balloon Fun

Concept: Visual-Motor Coordination
Purpose: To keep a balloon in the air for as long as possible
Situation: Leisure time
Materials: A big, round balloon

Activity: Blow up the balloon. Ask your child to keep the balloon in the air by hitting it repeatedly with one or two fingers. Have her count the number of hits she used to keep the balloon in the air.

Variation: Try to keep the balloon in the air by hitting it off certain body parts such as the hips, back, feet, or head. You can also try hitting it over a net or rope as in volleyball.

          26

46. Pouring

Concept: Visual-Motor Coordination
Purpose: To gain skill in pouring liquids
Situation: In the kitchen
Materials: A variety of tumblers, jars, and pitchers suitable for pouring; food coloring or soap

Activity: If your child can use a step ladder and work in the sink, you can avoid potential spills. Simply provide the pitchers, containers, and the water, and your child will have hours of fun. For added interest, add a few drops of food coloring or soap to the water.

47. Braiding

Concepts: Visual-Motor Coordination, Right and Left
Purpose: To learn to braid
Situation: Leisure time
Materials: Three colors of thick yarn or twine, tape

Activity: To teach your child to braid, cut equal lengths of colored yarn. Tie them in a knot at one end and tape the knot to the edge of a table or counter. (This set-up allows your child to manipulate the yarn easily.) When your child has finished braiding, tie off the ends and use for belts, bracelets, hair ribbons, or doll clothes.

48. Walk the Line

Concept: Visual-Motor Coordination
Purpose: To walk on a line by placing one foot directly in front of the other
Situation: Anywhere there is a line available on a walking surface
Materials: None

Activity: Have your child balance on the "tightrope" for as long as he can. Use a branch, stick, or umbrella as part of the "act." To challenge your child, use the cracks on the sidewalk and turn the corners on the lines that are perpendicular to each other.

49. Ring Toss

Concept: Visual-Motor Coordination
Purpose: To toss with accuracy
Situation: In the kitchen
Materials: Jar rubbers or rings (as used when canning), kitchen chair

Activity: Turn a kitchen chair upside down. Let your child toss the jar rubbers or rings so that they land on the chair legs

50. Mother May I *and* Simon Says

Concepts: Visual-Motor Coordination, Right and Left
Purpose: To follow directions and to imitate actions using direction words
Situation: Leisure time, outdoors
Materials: None

Activity: Play these old-time favorite games, concentrating on difficult motor tasks and right and left directionality. For example: "Mother, may I take three baby steps to the right?" "No, but you may take two giant steps to the left." Or "Simon says put your right hand on your left ear, and your left hand on your right ear."

51. Macaroni Necklaces

Concepts: Visual-Motor Coordination,
   Patterns, Sequencing
Purpose: To string a necklace or bracelet
Situation: Leisure time
Materials: Any kind of macaroni with a
   large hole; string, yarn, or shoelace; tape
   or glue; food coloring; rubbing alcohol

Activity: To color the macaroni, place the
desired amount in a jar, along with ½ teaspoon
of alcohol and a few drops of food
coloring. Shake the jar until the macaroni is
coated, then let dry on waxed paper (about
15 minutes). For easy threading, make a tip
on the yarn or string by wrapping a piece of
tape tightly around one end. Or dip the end
in glue and let dry. Let your child string the
macaroni, being careful to tie on the first and
last "bead." (Leave some string at each end
for tying.) You can encourage your child to
make patterns by repeating color sequences
over and over. Caution: Rubbing alcohol
should not be tasted or eaten.

WRITING

Writing stories and poems certainly requires creativity and inspiration. Writing is also a skill that improves with practice. Give your child plenty of opportunity for practice by writing birthday cards, letters to relatives, diaries of trips taken, and stories to accompany pictures. In the beginning, have your child dictate her story to you while you write it down. Sound out the words as you write them down and make your printing large and legible so that your child can read the words back to you. Once your child has an understanding of the association between the spoken and written word, and a beginning understanding of letter sounds, she may be ready to do her own writing. As your child writes, encourage her to sound out the words slowly, writing down the letter sounds that she hears. In the beginning, your child will probably omit vowels, consonant blends, and silent letters, so that the word *space* may be written as *sps*. That's okay! At this age, your child should only be expected to write the letter sounds that she knows and hears in the word. As your child's knowledge of phonics increases, so will her ability to spell. After your child has finished writing, you may want to go over it with her. If you feel that she has not written down sounds she knows, you may want to point that out. However, it is not necessary or even beneficial to correct the spelling of every word. If you want a perfectly spelled product, write the words down on a separate piece of paper and let your child copy them. Reading and writing are complementary skills—as one improves, so does the other.

IF YOUR CHILD IS READING

Here are some tips for parents whose children are reading when they enter kindergarten or who learn during the year.

1) Help your child along as he reads. Tell him the words he doesn't know if they cannot be sounded out easily. Beginning readers need plenty of assistance so that they can move along and maintain interest. Consult your child's teacher for a sense of what letter sounds or sight words you should expect your child to know, and those that your child is ready to learn.

2) Listen to your child as she tells you about what she has read. Question her about which part she liked best or how the story ended. When she talks about what she has read, it shows that she has understood. Reading without understanding is merely sounding out words.

3) Have your child read to you. Encouraging him to read the story to himself before he reads it to you will promote greater understanding and confidence. As your child reads to you, encourage him to take note of the punctuation marks, such as periods, question marks, and exclamation points, and to use the proper expression in his voice.

4) Keep a wide variety of reading materials in your home. Read the comics together in the daily newspaper. Interest your child in reading magazines by providing him with his own subscription. (*Ranger Rick* or *Highlights* are

wonderfully appealing to young children.) Get involved in a book club that mails out its selections. The arrival of books or magazines mailed directly to your child will provide a strong inducement to read. Even children who can only recognize a few words will enjoy picking them out of their own books. Your local library is an excellent source for beginning readers. Look for those books, such as the Dr. Seuss books, that have the words "Easy Reader" or "An I Can Read Book" printed on the cover.

5) Read anywhere and everywhere. Cereal boxes, labels in the supermarket, record album covers, and newspapers are just some of the materials that surround your child every day. Use them! Read. Let your child see you reading. Children learn by imitating.

6) Even if your child frequently reads on his own, it is still important for you to read to him on a regular basis.

MATHEMATICS

COUNTING WITH MEANING

To help your child learn to count with meaning, you should emphasize that each item is only to be touched once. Model this behavior by counting things for him at first. Instead of just handing your child 3 cookies, point to each one as you say, "one, two, three cookies." "We need four knives for the table. One, two, three, four." When you feel your child has begun to grasp the concept, try some of the following activities, doing the counting with your child.

52. Sound Counting

Concept: Counting with Meaning
Purpose: To count each object as it falls into a container
Situation: Leisure time
Materials: Metal pan or cup; 10–20 metal washers, buttons, dried beans

Activity: Tell your child to drop the objects into the pan one at a time, counting each time she hears the sound of the object hitting the pan.

53. Bouncing Ball

Concepts: Counting with Meaning, Skip Counting
Purpose: To bounce and catch a ball while counting to ten, twenty, or more—one count for each bounce
Situation: Outside
Materials: Large ball

Activity: Have your child bounce and catch a ball, counting as high as he can.

Variation: Try counting backwards, starting from ten. Or try skip counting—2, 4, 6, 8, 10; 5, 10, 15, 20, 25; 10, 20, 30, 40, 50. This activity may also be done with a jump rope or a balloon.

54. Dominoes

Concept: Counting with Meaning
Purpose: To count and match the numbers of dots on dominoes
Situation: Leisure time
Materials: Set of dominoes

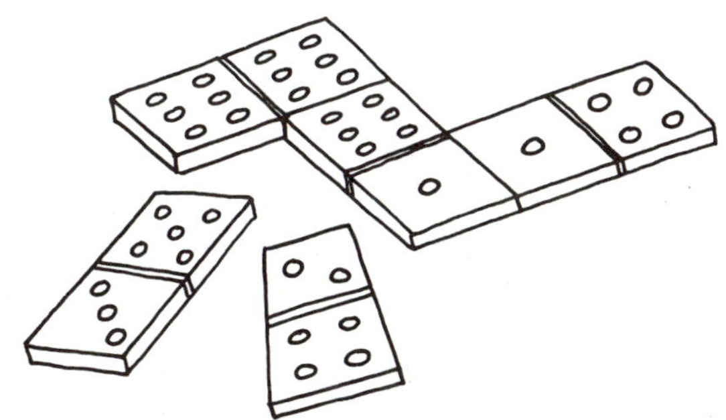

Activity: Pass out the dominoes, leaving ten in a drawing pile. The player with the double six begins the game by laying out the dominoes. The game is played by laying one side of a domino from your hand to a matching side already on the table. To lay down a domino, it must match only the exposed ends of the domino line. No score is kept. If you do not have a match, you must draw a domino from the pile. The player who runs out of dominoes first is the winner. This game can certainly be played by its regular rules with kindergarten children if your child is interested and ready.

55. Walk (skip, jump, march) and Count

Concept: Counting with Meaning
Purpose: To count while jumping, walking, skipping, etc.
Situation: Outdoors
Materials: None

Activity: If you are spending time outdoors with your child, let him try hopping on each sidewalk square, marching, skipping, or jumping rope. Ask him to count each time he takes a step.

56. How Many Now?

Concepts: Counting with Meaning, Counting On, Skip Counting, Addition
Purpose: To count by adding one more to the existing number
Situation: Leisure time
Materials: Any of the following: dried beans, pennies, poker chips, peanuts, raisins, animal crackers

Activity: To begin this activity, give your child one object and ask her how many she has. Give her another object, and ask how many she has now. Keep giving one more and repeating the question "One more— How many do you have now?" If she forgets, have her count the pile she has and then add one more.
Variation I: Write down the addition problem each time you add an object—$1 + 1 = 2$, $2 + 1 = 3$, $3 + 1 = 4$, etc.

Variation II: Try this activity with skip counting (counting by 2's, 5's, or 10's). Begin by placing the items into many piles of twos (or fives or tens). If you have small paper cups, you can put two (or five or ten) items in each cup, then play the game as before. Start with two and give your child two more, asking "How many now?" (4). "Two more, how many now?" (6), etc.

57. Egg Carton Counting

Concepts: Counting with Meaning, Number Recognition
Purpose: To match the correct number of objects to the written number
Situation: Leisure time
Materials: Empty egg carton, dried beans, marking pen

Activity: Write the numbers from one to ten, in order, on the back wall of each section of the egg carton. Store the beans in the other two sections. Have your child count out the number of beans for each section according to the written number. If he has counted correctly, there should be no beans left over. Vary the activity by starting with 10 and going backwards.

58. Number Hopscotch

Concepts: Number Recognition, Counting
with Meaning
Purpose: To count correctly the number of
fingers held up
Situation: Outdoors
Materials: Piece of chalk, sidewalk or
driveway

<table>
<tr><td>1</td><td>2</td><td>3</td></tr>
<tr><td>4</td><td>5</td><td>6</td></tr>
<tr><td>7</td><td>8</td><td>9</td></tr>
</table>

Activity: Draw a square and divide it into
nine sections. Write the numbers 1–9 in the
square, one in each section. Choose a
number and hold up that many fingers. Your
child must count how many fingers you are
holding up and jump to the proper square.
Being able to instantly recognize how many
fingers are being held up is an important
pre-addition and subtraction skill that all
children should learn.

59. Supermarket Math

Concepts: Concept of Less, Number
Recognition, Number Values,
Comparisons
Purpose: To find familiar numbers at the
supermarket
Situation: Grocery shopping
Materials: None

Activity: This activity is appropriate for
those children ready to learn to recognize
numbers up to 100 and beyond. Have your
child read you the prices on the items in the
supermarket. You may ask your child to
comparison shop by selecting the item that
costs the least. Or, ask your child to select
an item that costs less than a certain
amount. Show your child the number on a
can or box that indicates the weight of the
item and ask him to find the can or box that
contains a certain amount. Show your child
the scale that weighs produce, then let him
weigh the items and read the scale. When
you get home, have your child try to match
the prices on the items with the prices on the
receipt. This activity is guaranteed to make
your shopping take twice as long, but it is
most educational, and your child will begin to
learn the value of money.

60. Number Books

Concepts: Number Recognition, Counting
with Meaning
Purpose: To match a set of objects to the
corresponding number
Situation: Leisure time
Materials: Old magazines, scissors,
stapler, glue, paper, crayons

Activity: Make a booklet of blank pages by
stapling ten sheets of paper together along
one edge. Write the numerals from one to
ten, one at the top of each page. Have your
child look through the magazines, cutting out
one object for the number one page, two
objects for the number two page, etc. Have
him glue the pictures on the page as he
goes along. Have your child give the book a
title when finished.

61. Dot-to-Dots

Concepts: Number Recognition, Counting, Skip Counting, Counting Backwards

Purpose: To connect written numbers in their sequence

Situation: Leisure time

Materials: Dot-to-dot puzzle books are available in drug, toy, or book stores. Look for easy puzzles that have numbers 1–10 or 1–20.

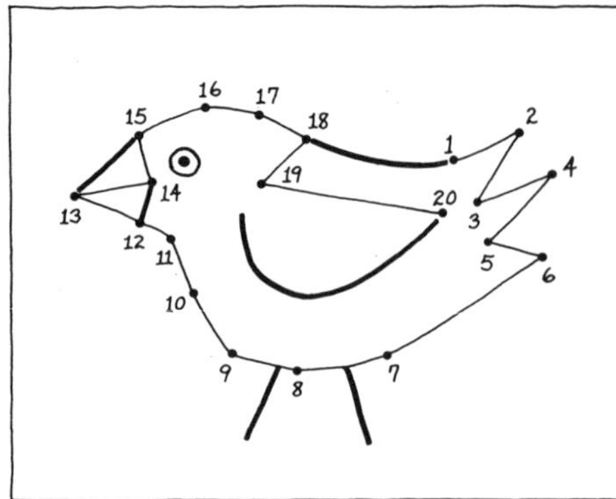

Activity: Dot-to-dot puzzles will entertain children for hours. They will also help to teach them the sequence of numbers.

Variation: Have your child count backwards, starting from the ten and counting the dots back to one. Dot-to-dots that use higher numbers (to 100 and beyond) and skip counting can be found in teacher supply stores.

62. Cornmeal Numbers

Concepts: Number Writing, Number Recognition

Purpose: To write numerals

Situation: Working in the kitchen, leisure time

Materials: yellow cornmeal—about $\frac{3}{4}$ cups, cookie sheet with sides

(See Cornmeal Letters language arts activity for directions.)

63. Sand Numbers

Concepts: Number Writing, Number Recognition

Purpose: To recognize and form the numbers

Situation: Leisure time

Materials: Glue, sand, thin cardboard, crayons

Activity: Write the numerals from one to nine, one each on pieces of thin cardboard. Squeeze glue onto the numerals, then have your child drop sand onto the glue. Excess sand can be brushed away when the numeral is dry. Draw arrows on the cardboard indicating the order with which the numeral is formed. Encourage your child to feel the number as he traces it with his fingers. You can also have him do a rubbing of the numeral by placing a sturdy piece of paper over the cardboard and rubbing with the side of a crayon. This activity can also be done with letters.

64. Water Painting

Concepts: Number Writing, Number Recognition

Purpose: To practice forming letters

Situation: Outdoors

Materials: Paint brush, pail of water

Activity: Water painting is the cleanest mess your child will ever make. This activity is best done on a warm day so that the sun can do the cleaning up. Give your child the brush, pail of water, and plenty of sidewalk space. She can practice numbers, letters, or just be creative.

65. How Many Are Left?

Concepts: Counting With Meaning, Counting Backwards, Subtraction, Concept of Less
Purpose: To subtract one object from an existing pile and tell how many are left
Situation: Leisure time
Materials: Any of the following: dried beans, pennies, poker chips, peanuts, raisins, animal crackers

Activity: Have your child start with 10 objects. Take one away and ask how many he has left. Keep repeating the activity while saying, "Now I'm going to take one away. You have one less. How many do you have left?" (Or let your child take them away himself and eat them each time, if edible.) If your child cannot easily count backwards, he may have to count the pile each time you take one away, but he should gradually get the idea. It may help to have a number line available so that your child can refer to it.

Variation: To make this activity more advanced, write the subtraction problems as you do them. For example, if you have a pile of 6 and you take 1 away, the equation would be written as $6 - 1 = 5$. After you have written a series of equations ($6 - 5 = 1$, $5 - 1 = 4$, $4 - 1 = 3$, etc.), have your child look at them to find a pattern.

66. War

Concepts: Number Values, Comparisons
Purpose: To decide which number is larger
Situation: Leisure time
Materials: Deck of playing cards with the picture cards removed

Activity: Divide the deck evenly between 2 players. Have each player stack her cards face down on the table. The players then turn over one card and compare them. The player with the highest value card takes the pair. If the two cards are the same, there is a "war." The players each put out 3 more cards, facedown, and turn up the fourth card. The player with the highest card in the "war" takes all the cards played in that trick. When one player wins all the cards, the game is over. As your child improves at this game, you may wish to include picture cards.

67. Raisin Monster

Concepts: Addition and Subtraction, Counting On
Purpose: To gain experience with the combinations of various numbers
Situation: Leisure time
Materials: Snack-size box of raisins

Activity: Begin the game by giving your child 3 raisins. Say, "Once there was a raisin monster. She loved to eat raisins! First she had three, then she took two more. (Let your child take two raisins from the box). How many raisins did the monster have altogether? . . . But the raisin monster was hungry, so she ate four of the raisins (your child eats four raisins). How many raisins did she have left? . . . But poor raisin monster—she was still hungry! So Mrs. Monster gave her three more raisins. (Give your child three more raisins.) How many raisins does the raisin monster have now?" Continue the game, using totals up to seven or eight, until your child is full! Each time your child figures out the total, he should be using the skill of "counting on" ("three raisins in my hand and the monster took two more, that's three/four-five."—*Not* one-two-three/four-five).

Variation: This game lends itself nicely to recording the addition and subtraction equations as you do them. ("Four raisins in your hand and the monster took two more, that's $4 + 2 = 6$, then the raisin monster ate three of them for breakfast, that's $6 - 3 = 3$.")

68. Hide the Beans

Concepts: Addition and Subtraction, Counting On
Purpose: To gain experience with the combinations that make up various numbers (5 is made up of 3 + 2, 0 + 5, 4 + 1, etc. . . .).
Situation: Leisure time
Materials: Small paper or plastic bowl, dried lima beans

Activity: This activity gets its benefit from being played many times with a variety of numbers. Using only 4 beans in the beginning, hide some under the bowl and place the rest on top. Your child is to guess how many beans are still hiding. To do this, have your child look at how many beans are on top of the bowl. Then have him recall how many you originally started with. With this information, your child should be able to detect how many beans are hiding under the bowl. If your child finds this too difficult, try working with three objects. If he succeeds, try other combinations, then move on to 4 beans. As your child improves at this game, show him how to record the equations, thus

is written as 3 + 2 = 5. (Don't forget to use the "counting on" trick to figure out the total!)

69. Green Pea Math

Concepts: Addition, Counting On
Purpose: To record the number combinations found in pea pods
Situation: Leisure time
Materials: Fresh pea pods, pencil, paper

Activity: To begin this activity, give your child five or six pea pods. Have her open up the pea pods and look at how many peas lie in each side of the pod. Then record the combinations. Thus, a pea pod that looks like this

will be written as: 3 + 4 = 7. Have your child use counting on to figure the totals.

70. Dice Toss

Concepts: Addition, Counting On
Purpose: To add together the number of dots on two dice
Situation: Leisure time
Materials: Two dice with one to six dots on the sides, pencil, paper

Activity: Let your child toss the dice, then record the combinations that turn up. Thus,

is written 3 + 5 = 8. (Have your child use counting on to figure the totals.)

71. Word Problems

Concept: Addition and Subtraction
Purpose: To complete math problems
   without the aid of concrete objects
Situation: Traveling in the car, leisure time
Materials: None

Activity: The use of real-life objects in addition and subtraction is a most important first step and should not be passed over by *any* child. However, once your child grasps the concepts of addition and subtraction, try doing some word problems. The crucial factor in doing word problems is to have your child form a mental picture of the story. You may begin by recreating some of the games you have previously played. ("Imagine that you are opening a pea pod. There are two peas on one side and three on the other. How many altogether?" Or, "Pretend that you have tossed two dice. There is one dot on one dice and four on the other. How many dots altogether?") Then, try making up addition and subtraction problems that may occur in your child's everyday life. ("There are four people in our family and you bring two friends home for dinner. How many places should you set at the table?" Or, "I brought home six doughnuts from the bakery and your father ate two of them. How many are left?")

72. Cereal Patterns

Concept: Patterns
Purpose: To string a pattern
Situation: Leisure time
Materials: Two or three types of breakfast
   cereals—Cheerios, Spoon-Size Shredded
   Wheat, and Puffed Rice will work well;
   large, blunt needle; thread

Activity: A pattern is any sequence that repeats itself. Double-thread the needle and tie a piece of cereal at the end to serve as a knot. Have your child string an initial pattern, such as one Cheerio, one Shredded Wheat, and one Puffed Rice. Then help him to continue that pattern the length of the thread. Your child can wear the pattern as a necklace or bracelet, eating cereal whenever the hunger pangs take over!

Variation: Patterns also can be created by stringing beads, using pegboards, or building block towers. Encourage your child to look for patterns in clothing, architecture, and nature.

73. How Tall Am I?

Concepts: Comparisons, Measuring
Purpose: To use measuring skills and the
   concept of *taller/shorter*
Situation: Leisure time
Materials: Yardstick, pencil

Activity: Find a section of wall space in your house that you do not mind marking on. About once every two months, measure your child's height, marking a line with a pencil and adding the date. Show your child how many inches or centimeters tall he is on a yardstick, then let him measure his height with hands, blocks, or anything else available. Measuring with common objects, such as blocks, will be more relevant to your child than inches or centimeters. Remind him that, when measuring, you match the edge of your measuring device with the edge of the object you are measuring. Thus, if you are measuring with blocks, place the first block on the floor and the next block right up to the first, neither overlapping nor leaving space in between. Your child will be delighted to see his growth charted so carefully and will enjoy comparing the different heights.

74. Measuring with Feet

Concepts: Comparisons, Measuring
Purpose:　To measure length
Situation:　Leisure time
Materials:　None

Activity: Show your child how to measure length by putting one foot right in front of the other and counting steps. Have your child guess what the longest item in your living room might be and then measure it. Now find the shortest item in the room and measure it. Can she figure out how much longer the one item is than the other? Can she find things in the room that are equal in length? Can she measure round things using this method? Are there things she can't measure using this method? This activity lends itself to many variations. Your child will not only enjoy the measuring, but the balancing act that it requires as well.

Variation: Have your child stand on a piece of cardboard or stiff paper and trace around his feet. Let him cut the feet out and use them as rulers to measure things he was not able to measure by the walking method, such as tables, walls, himself, etc. You can also trace around and cut out your own feet. Let your child measure the same item with both sets of feet. Why is there a difference?

75. Just Right

Concepts: Comparisons, Measuring,
　Concept of Less
Purpose:　To understand the concept of
　less
Situation:　Mealtime
Materials:　None

Activity: The concepts of *less* and *least* are often very difficult for young children to grasp. When dishing out food for dinner, let your child help you. If she puts too many potatoes on the plate, tell her it is too much—that you want her to have *less*. Let

her spoon some back until it is "just right." When you sit down ask your child which person at the table has the *most* potatoes. Then ask her who has the *least*. If you continue to pair the concepts of *less* and *least* with their opposites *more* and *most,* your child will soon add those words to her vocabulary.

76. Jars

Concepts: Comparisons, Visual-Motor
　Coordination
Purpose:　To match lids to jars
Situation:　Leisure time
Materials:　8–12 jars of varying diameters
　with screw-top lids

Activity: Let your child unscrew the jar lids, mix them up, and put them back on again. She may also enjoy putting the jars or lids in order from largest to smallest.

77. Yarn Shapes

Concept:　Shape
Purpose:　To create shapes using yarn
Situation:　Leisure time
Materials:　Yarn, glue, cardboard

Activity: Let your child create familiar shapes by glueing the yarn onto cardboard. When dry, your child can trace his finger over the yarn as a tactile reference to the shapes he is learning.

78. Shape Hunt

Concept: Shapes
Purpose: To find familiar shapes
Situation: Traveling in the car, indoors, outdoors, shopping
Materials: None

Activity: Pick a shape, such as triangle, that your child is having difficulty recalling. Let him trace his fingers around various triangular objects. Discuss how many sides and points the triangle has. When you go out, see how many triangles you and your child can spot.

79. Shape Pictures

Concept: Shapes
Purpose: To create pictures using cut-out shapes
Situation: Leisure time
Materials: Circles, squares, triangles, and rectangles cut from colored construction paper, glue, cardboard

Activity: Let your child create a picture or design using the cut-out shapes. After arranging the shapes on the cardboard, she can glue them down.

80. Shape Sorting

Concepts: Shapes, Sorting
Purpose: To sort shapes that are alike into piles
Situation: Leisure time
Materials: Any set of materials that contains circles, triangles, squares, and rectangles. You can use building blocks, shapes cut from cardboard, or any variety of items collected from around the house.

Activity: Before your child begins sorting the shapes, discuss the qualities of each one. You might say, "How many sides does the square have? How many corners? Can you think of something that is shaped like a square? How are squares different from rectangles?" After sorting the shapes into 4 piles, see if your child can recall the names of all of the shapes.

81. Sorting Buttons

Concept: Sorting and Classifying
Purpose: To sort buttons according to similarities and differences
Situation: Leisure time
Materials: 20 – 30 odd buttons, egg carton

Activity: Let your child sort the buttons into the egg carton sections in any way that she chooses. Afterwards, discuss why she chose to sort them the way she did. Then ask her if there might be a different way to do it. For example, if your child has sorted the buttons by color, you might next direct her attention to the texture of the buttons. Encouraging your child to complete the activity in a variety of ways will help to develop flexible and creative thinking.

82. Clean-up

Concept: Sorting and Classifying
Purpose: To sort items into like categories
Situation: In the kitchen, in the child's room
Materials: A messy house

Activity: Make clean-up a learning activity by having your child sort and put away the silverware, help put the groceries away, and sort and categorize toys and clothing.

83. Card Sorting

Concept: Sorting and Classifying
Purpose: To sort a deck of cards according to the number, color, or suit
Situation: Leisure time
Materials: Deck of playing cards

Activity: Give your child a deck of cards and ask him to "put the ones that are alike together." Allow him to figure out a way to do that (by number, suit, or color). After doing it one way, ask your child if he can figure out a different way to do it.

84. Let's Go

Concept: Sorting and Classifying
Purpose: To increase classification skills through imagination
Situation: Traveling in the car
Materials: None

Activity: Begin this game by picking a place to go on an imaginary trip. You might say, "Let's go to the airport. I see an airplane." Your child may respond with "I see lots of people at the airport." Continue this way until you exhaust the possibilities, then choose a different place to go.

85. Estimation Games

Concept: Estimation, Counting, Skip Counting
Purpose: To increase estimation skills
Situation: At home, traveling, at the supermarket
Materials: Large number of objects

Activity: Estimation can be done informally in a wide variety of situations. Make it a family or party game. Here are some suggestions.
1) Estimate the number of marshmallows or peanuts in a bag, raisins in a box, grapes in a bunch, or chips in a chocolate chip cookie.
2) Estimate how many miles to school, church, shopping, or grandma's house.
3) Estimate how many pounds the meat, potatoes, apples, or oranges will weigh at the supermarket.
4) Estimate how many pages in a book, toys in a chest, or socks in a drawer. To check her guess, have your child try counting the items by 2's, 5's, or 10's.

86. Listen for the Bell

Concept: Telling Time
Purpose: To experience how long an hour is
Situation: Leisure time
Materials: Timer with a bell

Activity: When the clock strikes the hour, set your timer for one hour. When the bell goes off, tell your child that one hour has passed, and show him how far the hands of the clock have moved. Doing this a number of times will help give your child a clearer idea of the length of an hour. This activity can be done with any unit of time.

87. Making Your Own Clock

Concept: Telling Time
Purpose: To make a model clock and learn about its use
Situation: Leisure time
Materials: Paper plate with circles drawn where the numbers should be, minute and hour hands cut from heavy paper or cardboard, paper fastener, pen

Activity: Help your child draw the numbers in the circles and fasten the hands onto the paper plate. Begin by teaching your child to read the hours. You may wish to relate the hours to the times that your child eats meals, goes to school, or goes to bed by copying the time from the real clock to the paper clock.

88. Events Calendar

Concept: Calendars
Purpose: To become familiar with the calendar
Situation: Leisure time
Materials: Large paper calendar

Activity: Post the calendar in a spot where your child will see it every day, such as the refrigerator. Write down special activities that are coming up, such as birthday parties and trips. Each morning at breakfast, discuss the day and the date. In the evening, your child can cross off the day before he goes to bed.

89. Value of Coins

Concept: Coins
Purpose: To recognize and understand the value of pennies, nickels, dimes, and quarters
Situation: Leisure time, shopping
Materials: Coins

Activity: If your child understands the concepts of addition, subtraction, counting on, and counting by fives, he is ready to learn the value of coins. Begin by discussing the value of nickels and pennies, then have your child make combinations such as 7¢ and 11¢. Next discuss dimes, then continue asking your child to make up combinations such as 10¢, 15¢, and 18¢. Make sure you discuss all the different ways you can make each combination (18¢ can be made by one dime, one nickel, and three pennies; or three nickels and three pennies; or 18 pennies). Continue on to quarters and half-dollars, if your child is able.

Variation: Once your child understands the value of coins, try playing "store." Take several items from the kitchen, mark them with a price (if there is not one already) and have your child count up the proper amount in change.

90. Mancala

Concept: Games
Purpose: To play the game Mancala
Situation: Leisure time
Materials: Egg carton, 48 dried lima
   beans, two paper cups

Activity: Mancala is an ancient game that takes many forms in a variety of cultures. To play this variation, place four beans in each section of the egg carton. The object of the game is to capture your opponent's beans. Your beans are those in the six sections on your side of the egg carton, and your opponent's are on the opposite side. Moves are made by picking up *all* the beans in one section and dropping them, one in each section, and moving around the "board" in a counter-clockwise direction.

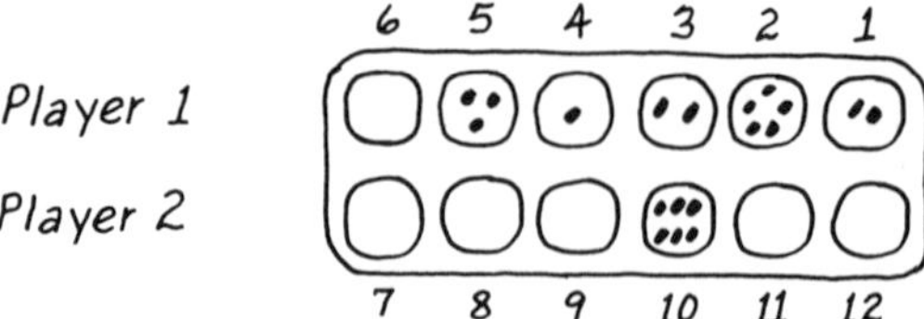

Thus, if you pick up all the beans from section #10 (and there are 4 beans in that section) you drop them into sections #11, #12, #1, and #2. You must pick up all the beans in a section and drop them, one in each section beginning with the next section, going around the board until you run out of beans. (Note: You will be dropping beans on your opponent's side of the board. However, you may only pick up beans from your side of the board.) If, when you drop your beans into an opponent's section, there are only one or two beans already in the section, you may capture them. Take your opponent's one or two beans (and your own, which you dropped in) and place them in your paper cup. They are now yours to keep until the end of the game. (Note: You may only capture your opponent's beans if there are one or two in the section and only in a

section into which you dropped the last bean in your hand. Thus, if the board looked like this:

you could pick up the 6 beans in your section #10 and drop them in the next six sections until you finished up in your opponents #4 section. You may then capture the beans in the #4 section and also the beans in #3 section because there are two of them and because they are next to the #4 section, which you were able to capture. Thus, you may capture any section (with one or two beans) that precedes the section that you dropped your last bean into. You could then capture the beans in sections #4 and 5, but not those in #1 because it is separated by section #2, which has five beans. Play is over when all the beans have been captured. The person with the most beans is the winner.

   This game is really very simple to learn. Strategies, however, can range from the very simple to the complex. Mancala is a most entertaining game for players age 5 to adults.

Other games for ages 5 and up:
   Checkers
   Othello
   Chinese checkers
   Uno

SOCIAL STUDIES/SCIENCE/HEALTH

The following are suggestions for experiments to try and trips to take that will stimulate your child and complement the kindergarten curriculum. They are also suitable for rainy day activities and groups of children.

91. Making Butter

Materials ½ pint whipping cream, clear jar with lid, crackers

Activity: Pour cream into the jar and close the lid tightly. Let your child shake the jar vigorously. Within 6–7 minutes, the cream will turn to butter before your eyes. Let your child taste the buttermilk that has separated from the butter. Spread the fresh butter on the crackers and enjoy. Delicious!

92. How Did You Do That?

Materials: Small balloon, soda pop or catsup bottle, cider or apple vinegar, baking soda, teaspoon

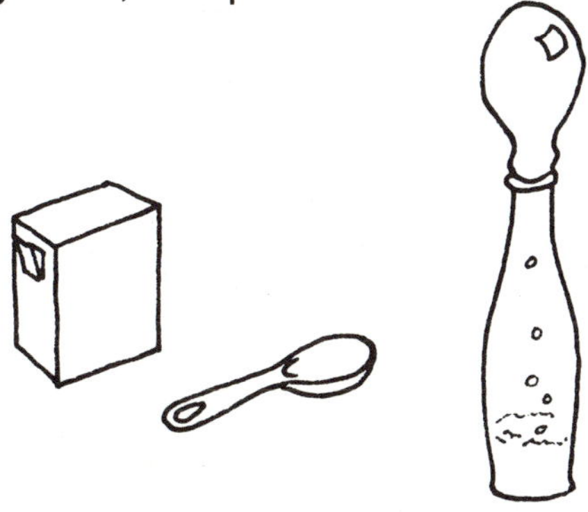

Activity: Pour about an inch of the vinegar into the bottle. Put 2 teaspoons of baking soda inside the bottle, then quickly slip the open end of the balloon over the neck of the bottle. The balloon should blow up from the gas you have created by combining the vinegar and baking soda.

93. Sail Away

Materials: Jar lid or walnut shell half, toothpicks, dab of clay or play dough, paper, scissors, crayons

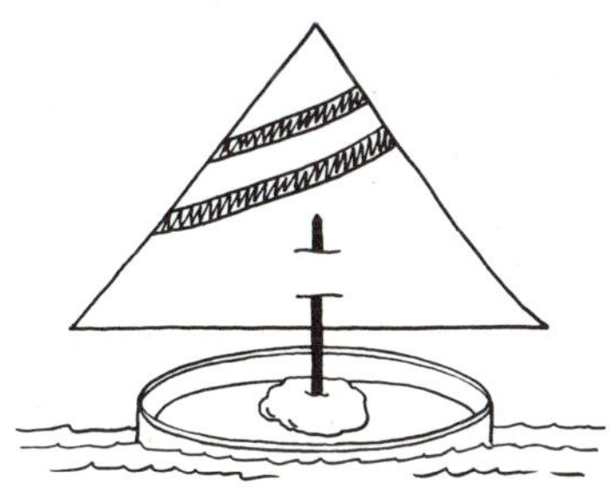

Activity: Have your child draw a small triangle or square sail on paper. Decorate the sail with the crayons, then cut it out. Poke the top of the toothpick through the sail and the bottom half into the clay. Stick the clay into the jar lid, and you have a very seaworthy boat. Just blow on the sail and watch it scoot away! For added fun, make several boats, each one with a different shape sail, then have a race in your bathtub. Which sail worked best?

94. Color Mixing

Materials: Yellow, blue, and red food coloring, eye dropper, white styrofoam egg carton, water

Activity: Fill three of the egg cups with water and squirt the red, blue, and yellow food coloring into the water. Show your child how to work the eye dropper, then let him go to work, sucking up colored water from one egg cup, squirting it into another and mixing the colored water. What results is an intriguing lesson in colors, without the messy clean-up.

95. **Your Own Garden**

Materials: Glass jar, paper towels, dried lima beans

Activity: Soak the beans overnight to ensure rapid sprouting. The next day, line the jar with the paper towels. Place the beans between the towels and the side of the jar so that they may be seen. Put some water in the bottom of the jar, adding to it each day to keep the towels wet. Keep the jar in a sunny place. When the beans have sprouted good-sized leaves, they may be planted.

Variation I: Growing a Sweet Potato or Avocado Plant
Materials: Sweet potato with buds or an avocado pit that has already split, glass jar, toothpicks

Activity: Place four toothpicks into the sweet potato or avocado pit and place small-end down, into the mouth of the jar, letting the toothpicks rest on the edge. Add enough water to keep the bottom of the plant wet. Let your child check the level of the water every day to make sure that there is enough. Keep the jar in a sunny place.

Variation II: Growing Fruit Seeds
Materials: Seeds from lemons, oranges, apples, pears, etc.; paper cup or other container; soil

Activity: Let the seeds dry out for a few hours. Place soil into the container and plant the seed. Make sure to label the seeds if you are growing more than one kind. Water and watch them grow! (You may wish to plant several of each variety to ensure that one will come up.)

Variation III: Growing Carrot Tops
Materials: Carrot tops, small stones, saucer

Activity: Cut off the tops of some fresh carrots and put them cut-side-down in a saucer. Pile the stones around them to keep them in place. Always keep a little water in the dish. In a week, you will have plenty of "rabbit food!"

Variation IV: Growing a Sprout Salad
Materials: Alfalfa seeds, mung bean sprouts, dried lentils, and chick peas; glass jars

Activity: Place the beans separately in the jars and soak in water overnight. The next day, pour out the water and place jars in a dark place. Keep the beans away from the light for 2–3 days, rinsing once or twice daily (very important!). After 2–3 days, place the beans in a sunny place for 1–2 days, again rinsing daily. This allows the sprouts to develop chlorophyll. When the leaves of the beans are small but green, they are ready to eat. Spread on a salad and serve.

Variation V: Cut clippings from a plant in your house, such as a Swedish ivy or spider plant. Place the clippings in water for two weeks so that roots begin to grow, then plant the clippings. Tie a bow around the pot and give it as a gift to a special friend.

96. Using Your Senses

Materials: Small amounts of food for tasting, such as bread, mayonnaise, mustard, peanut butter, sour cream, butter, apples, crackers, chocolate, salt, sugar
Items for smelling, such as vanilla, coffee, catsup, lemon extract, soap, onion, spices

Activity: Place all the items on a tray and let your child see them. Then blindfold her, and give her items to taste and identify. Do the same with the items for smelling. If your child can identify all the items, try another experiment. Ask her to hold her nose and taste some of the items again. Is there a difference?

97. Silly Ice Cubes

Materials: Several unusual watertight containers that can be used as ice molds, such as a gelatin mold, eggshell, toy boat, and empty plastic tube

Activity: This activity demonstrates that water, shapeless when not contained in a vessel, can conform to any shape when frozen. Fill the containers with water and freeze. (You may also wish to add food coloring to the water.) When frozen, unmold by running warm water over the sides of the container. Watch the ice cubes to see which will melt first, or place them in a bowl of punch and serve at a party.

98. Shadow Simon Says

Materials: A sunny day

Activity: Take your child outside on a bright, sunny day and ask him to find his shadow. Discuss why we have shadows (the sunlight is blocked by your body). Is your shadow in front or in back of you? Is your shadow the same size and shape as your body? How is it different? Play a game of Simon Says, giving commands such as, "Simon says, 'Flap your arms.'" or "Simon says, 'Sit down.'" Make sure your child is watching his shadow as he does the actions.

Variation: Place a stick about 1½ feet tall into the ground. Observe the changes in the shadow cast by the stick at 10 AM, noon, 3 PM and 5 PM. Your child can make a record of the shadow at each interval. He may also wish to measure the length of the shadow at the different intervals and compare them.

99. My Family Tree

Materials: Large piece of paper, crayons

Activity: Help your child to draw a family tree, starting with the oldest living members of your family. The picture should include only those members of the family with which the child is acquainted. This activity will help your child to understand that "Uncle" or "Grandma" is not only a title, but a relationship.

100. Household Helper

Materials: A large piece of paper, crayons

Activity: Draw up a chart that depicts the household responsibilities of each member of your family. You may want to set it up on a weekly basis, so that your child becomes familiar with the days of the week and his responsibilities for each of the days.

101. What Can You See?

Materials: Pair of binoculars, tall building (at least 7 stories)

Activity: Try to find a building in your neighborhood from which you can get a good view of the surrounding area. Using the binoculars, locate familiar buildings, such as the grocery store, school, or park. See if your child can trace the route he walks or drives to school. If you have a local map, you can relate what you see to the symbols of the streets, parks, and buildings.

102. Telephone Directory

Materials: A home-made or commercially prepared address and phone book

Activity: Help your child to make her own phone book. You can include the phone numbers and addresses of friends and relatives. Use this activity to teach your child her own phone number and address, as well as polite phone manners and emergency procedures, such as dialing 911. You will also want to discuss the times of day when a phone call can be made, and long distance versus local calls.

103. First-Aid Box

Materials: Sturdy box, band aids, adhesive tape, sterile bandages, antiseptic, tweezers, scissors, sterilized needle, bacteria-killing soap

Activity: Gather the contents of the box together and discuss how and why each article is used. Let your child place them carefully in the box. Put the box in a prominent and accessible place in case of accident or injury. You will want to remind your child that the box is not a toy and should only be taken out when an adult is around.

104. Trips

Taking trips, whether large or small, planned or spontaneous, is one of the best ways to widen your child's store of experiences and enrich his understanding of the world. The following are merely suggestions meant to encourage you to use your imagination and local resources.

Bakery
Pet store
Hardware store
Florist
Supermarket (visit the loading docks and meat locker)
Health food store
Dry cleaners
Bank
Post office
Fire station
Police station
Newspaper office
Hospital
Railroad station
Airport
Harbor
On-going building and road construction sites
Zoo
Amusement park
Museums
Planetarium
Aquarium
Sporting events
Circus
Concerts
Dance productions
Farm
Dairy
City hall
Beach
Mountains
Theater

ART/MUSIC/DRAMA

The best way to expose your child to the various artistic media is simply to provide him with a basic set of materials. A short discussion on the proper care and use of the materials will be in order, so that your child does not express himself on your freshly painted living room walls. A basic set of materials might include:

set of 12 or more crayons
watercolor markers
colored pencils
watercolors
glue
scissors
drawing paper (Used computer print-out
   paper is great, and it's free. A sketch pad
   also works nicely.)
paper scraps (from tissue and wrapping
   paper, wallpaper samples, construction
   paper)
tempra paint (optional)

105. Crayon Resist

Materials: paper, crayons, watercolors

Activity: Have your child draw a picture with crayons. Make sure the marks are very dark and cover the paper well. Then wash over the whole picture (crayon included) with the watercolors. The crayon, because it is made of wax, will resist the watercolor. The wash will only take to the paper that has been left uncovered. The result is a picture with an interesting texture and design.

106. Painting with Food Coloring

Materials: Paper cups or ice cube tray, food coloring, water, Q-tips, paper

Activity: Fill the paper cups or ice cube tray with water and let your child add the food coloring. Use the Q-tips as paint brushes to paint a picture.

107. Crayon Rubbings

Materials: Crayons or chalk, paper

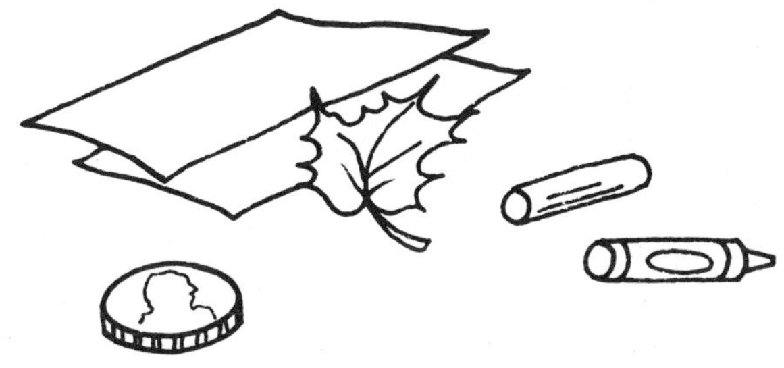

Activity: Look indoors and out for objects with an interesting texture. Items that have good surfaces for rubbings are: tires, straw baskets, burlap, leaves, brick wall, tree bark, grave stones, and corrugated paper. To make a rubbing of the item, place the paper on the surface and rub gently back and forth with the side of the crayon or chalk. If you have a large piece of paper, you can make rubbings of several different surfaces. Label each surface, or see if others can guess what they are.

108. Bubble Prints

Materials: Straws, bowl, dishwashing liquid, tempera paint, paper, tray or cookie sheet

Activity: Make up a batch of colored, bubbly water in a bowl by adding dishwashing liquid and small amount of tempera paint. Pour a little of the water in the tray. Give your child a straw and have her blow into the water to create frothy bubbles. Then place the paper face down on the bubbles and press gently. The result will be a print of the bubble design.

109. Straw Paintings

Materials: Straws, paper, thinned tempera paint

Activity: Place a small spoonful of thin tempera paint on a piece of paper. Give your child a straw and have him blow onto the dab of paint. If the paint is properly thinned, it should scoot across the paper, making interesting, spidery designs. The paint will dry quickly, allowing you to do several layers of paint in different colors.

110. Ink Blots

Materials: Tempera paint, paper, paint brushes

Activity: Fold the paper in half, open it up, and instruct your child to dab paint on one of the halves. Then fold the halves together and press. Open up the paper, and you will find a symmetrical design. Can you turn it into a butterfly?

111. Vegetable Prints

Materials: Tempera paint (not too thick); paint brushes; vegetables or fruits that have distinct designs when cut in half, such as oranges, apples, red cabbage, onions, celery; paper

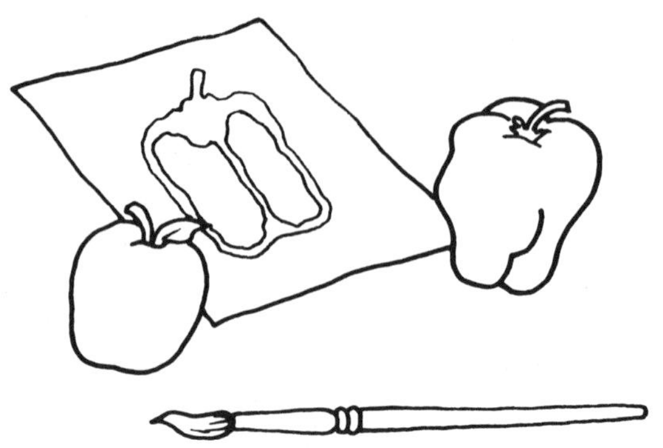

Activity: Brush the vegetable halves with paint and press onto the paper. You can print a pattern by repeating the design over and over.

112. Paper Chains

Materials: Paste or glue, paper strips (approximately 1″ × 4″) made from colored construction paper

Activity: To make the chains, simply take a strip of paper, bend it to make a circle and paste the ends together. Take a second strip and slip it through the first circle. Bend it to make another circle and paste the ends together. Keep doing this until the chain is the desired length. The chains can be used as necklaces and Christmas tree or party decorations.

113. Paper Bag Puppets

Materials: Small lunch bags or large grocery sacks, scissors, glue, paper scraps, crayons or markers

Activity: To make paper bag puppets, use the fold at the bottom of the bag as the mouth, and decorate the face using paper scraps for hair, eyebrows, and clothes. Draw in the facial features with crayons or markers. Make several puppets and put on a play!

To make child-sized costumes, use grocery sacks, cutting out holes for the eyes and arms. Decorate in the same fashion, making the features large and prominent. Material scraps and buttons can be used to simulate clothing and yarn can be used for the hair.

114. Make a Hideout or Fort

Materials: A large blanket or sheet, small table

Activity: Throw the blanket over the table so that you create a little "house." Let your child and a friend crawl inside with a few favorite toys, books, and a flashlight. Your child can pretend the hideaway is a fort, castle, cave, or spaceship.

115. Stick Puppets

Materials: Construction paper, crayons or markers, glue or tape, scissors, Popsicle sticks or toilet paper tubes

Activity: Outline and cut out a person, animal, or special storybook character from construction paper. Tape or glue the Popsicle stick or toilet paper tube to the back of the puppet for support, leaving enough room for a handle. Put on a puppet show using these and other puppets. Use two chairs with a blanket thrown over them for the stage.

116. Drum

Materials: Coffee can with lid, or oatmeal box; masking tape; spoon, pencil with eraser, or stick; yarn or string; construction paper (optional); crayons (optional)

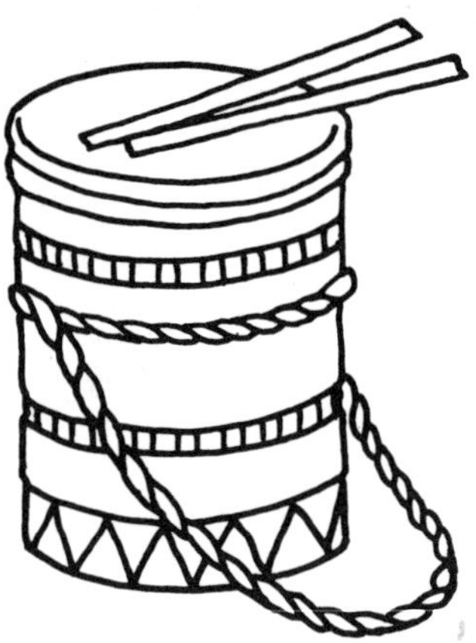

Activity: Secure the lid of the drum with tape. If you like, you can decorate the drum with construction paper and crayons, then tie the string or yarn around the coffee can and hang it around your child's neck. Let her use the stick, pencil or spoon as a drumstick.

117. Violin or Banjo

Materials: Sturdy shoe box with lid; rubber bands of different widths, large enough to fit around box; scissors

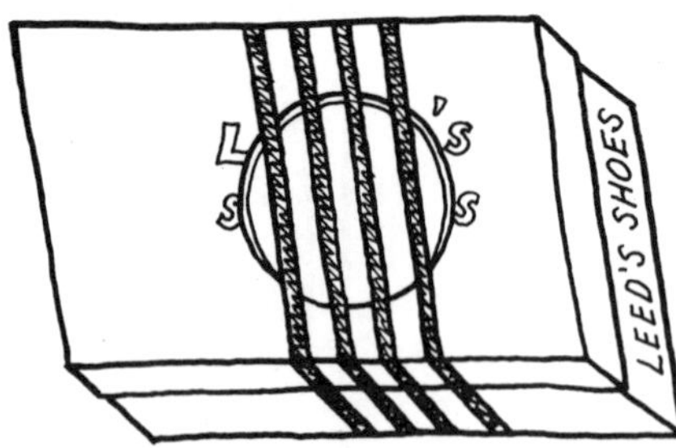

Activity: Cut a large round hole in the lid of the shoe box. Place lid on box and stretch the rubber bands around the box and over the hole. Show your child how to pluck the strings over the hole and listen to the sounds the different rubber bands make.

118. Maracas

Materials: Small frozen juice can; waxed paper; rubber band, dried beans, rice, or macaroni

Activity: Fill the container with a handful of beans, rice, or macaroni. Cover the open end with a square of waxed paper and secure it to the can with a rubberband or tape. Make several maracas, using the different substances to create different sounds.

119. Tambourine

Materials: Two paper plates or foil pie tins; dried beans, rice, or macaroni; masking tape or stapler

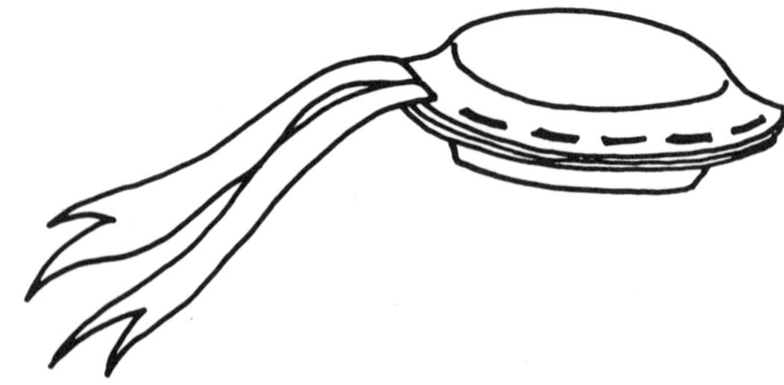

Activity: Put a handful of beans, rice, or macaroni in one of the plates. Lay the other plate face down over the first and tape or staple the edges together. Now shake! The tambourine can be decorated with paper streamers for a pretty effect.

PHYSICAL EDUCATION

As in art, simply providing your child with equipment will go a long way towards helping him/her develop coordination and control. A basic set of equipment might include:

> balls (football, round ball)
> jump rope
> hula hoop
> bicycle

> Some fun additions to this set would be:

> scooter
> stilts
> Frisbee
> bean bags

Allow your child plenty of opportunity to use his/her equipment, as well as neighborhood park or school climbing equipment. Try to discourage stereotyping certain sports skills as strictly masculine or feminine.

All children, especially those identified as having difficulties with large motor coordination and balance, will benefit from an after-school sport, gymnastic, or dance program. Children develop their attitudes towards physical fitness—and their ability to participate in these activities—at a very young age. It is never too early to begin a regular physical education program.

The following are some activities you may wish to try with your child or with a group of children.

120. Stick Steps

Purpose: To promote static and dynamic balance.
Materials: A collection of sticks or leaves from your yard

Activity: Scatter the sticks or leaves around a small area. Have your child move around the area by stepping only on the sticks (or leaves).
Variation: To do this activity indoors, use torn bits of paper.

121. Bow Legs

Purpose: To develop leg strength
Materials: Round ball of any type

Activity: Place a round ball between the knees and try to walk or hop. Try a variety of different sized balls, and see what kinds of walking styles they require.

122. Dodge and Catch

Purpose: To develop agility and hand-eye coordination
Materials: Beach ball or nerf ball

Activity: Have your child stand against a wall approximately six feet away. Your child should try to dodge your throw. If he is hit, it becomes his turn to throw the ball. This game is fun to play with a group of children.

123. Egghead

Purpose: To develop balance
Materials: 2 or 3 empty egg cartons

Activity: Place an egg carton with the open end down on your child's head. Then place a closed carton on top of the open one and have your child walk, gallop, or jog to a spot and come back.
Variation: Your child may enjoy being timed and working to improve his time. To make the activity more difficult, use 3 egg cartons instead of 2.

124. Frisbee Golf

Purpose: To promote hand-eye coordination, and develop an efficient throwing motion
Materials: Frisbee

Activity: Before playing Frisbee Golf, your child should spend some time learning to throw and catch the Frisbee. Frisbee Golf is played by keeping track of how many throws you make before you hit a specific target, and trying to hit a series of targets in sequence.

125. Hand Soccer

Purpose: To develop agility, hand-eye coordination, and balance
Materials: Round ball

Activity: The playing field in this game can be any size. Establish two "home base" or goal areas. The object of the game is to roll the ball on the ground with your hands, past your opponent and into your goal. Your opponent can try to take the ball away from you.

SOCIAL DEVELOPMENT

For some kindergarten children, getting along with peers in a large group situation can be a difficult experience. If your child is having trouble sharing or cooperating with others, he needs opportunities to develop his social skills in a structured situation. Invite one friend over and monitor the situation carefully. When problems arise, discuss ways in which they might be solved with mutual satisfaction. If both children want to be captain of the spaceship, ask them for suggestions that seem fair to both children—taking turns being captain, having two captains, each being captain of her own spaceship, playing a different game. Do not let the children resume their play until both agree upon a solution. Provide opportunities wherein cooperating will yield results that are more satisfactory than if the job or activity were done alone. Examples of such activities would be: constructing a large block structure, playing a card or board game, or building a fort or hide-away.

Make sure that your rules and expectations are clear and consistent. It is important to delineate just when certain behaviors are acceptable and when they are not. If your child talks when he should be listening, or is wild when he should be quiet, discuss with him when and where he is allowed to talk and be wild, so that he feels there are acceptable outlets for his natural impulses.

If your child is exhibiting a behavior problem at school, talk with his teacher. See if you can come up with a program that can be used both at home and at school so that your child is not receiving any mixed messages.

Appendix A

YOUR CHILD AND TELEVISION

Television, when used to inform, educate and entertain in a thoughtful manner, has almost unlimited potential. Unfortunately, the majority of prime-time programming is dedicated almost exclusively to a very superficial form of entertaining. Kindergarten-age children are very impressionable television viewers. They can take in and retain a great deal of information, but do not yet have the ability to discriminate between fantasy and reality. Children form their impressions of adult behavior through observation. Those children who watch a great deal of television will undoubtedly be influenced by the attitudes purveyed by television—attitudes that may differ widely with those of your family and community. In addition, the hours watching television are subtracted from the most important aspect of your child's education: life experience.

To remedy this situation, children must be taught to control television rather than letting it control them. To achieve this, begin by setting a limit of one or two shows a week on school nights, (homework and chores must be finished beforehand), and two nights of television (out of the three) on weekends. Then stick to your guns! Allow your children to select what they wish to watch at the beginning of the week. By choosing carefully in advance, your children will be developing responsibility for making decisions that are important to them. Your children will also be forming the habit of considering television to be only one of the many entertainment/learning tools available. When you can, watch these programs with your children. Afterwards, discuss what you have seen.

Of course, when you severely limit your children's television viewing, you also must make the commitment to fill that void. When used correctly, television can inform, educate and entertain. When used incorrectly, television can control your child and your family.

ALTERNATIVES TO TELEVISION

There are alternatives to television that, as well as entertaining and informing, will also increase listening skills and stimulate the imagination. These alternatives are: records, tape recorders, and radio drama. Records of children's rhymes and stories are often cherished by children as much as books. In addition to record and toy shops, local libraries often have extensive record collections that include recordings of great literature read aloud. Tape recorders offer many of the same benefits. Low-cost tapes accompanied by books, on which a narrator will read a story aloud, will provide hours of enjoyment for children. You or your child can also experiment with doing your own recording of stories, poems, and songs.

Unfortunately, there is very little radio drama left. For a minor contribution to your local public radio station, you will receive a program listing that will state when these shows are being broadcasted. They may be hard to find, but they are usually of the highest quality.

       54

Appendix B

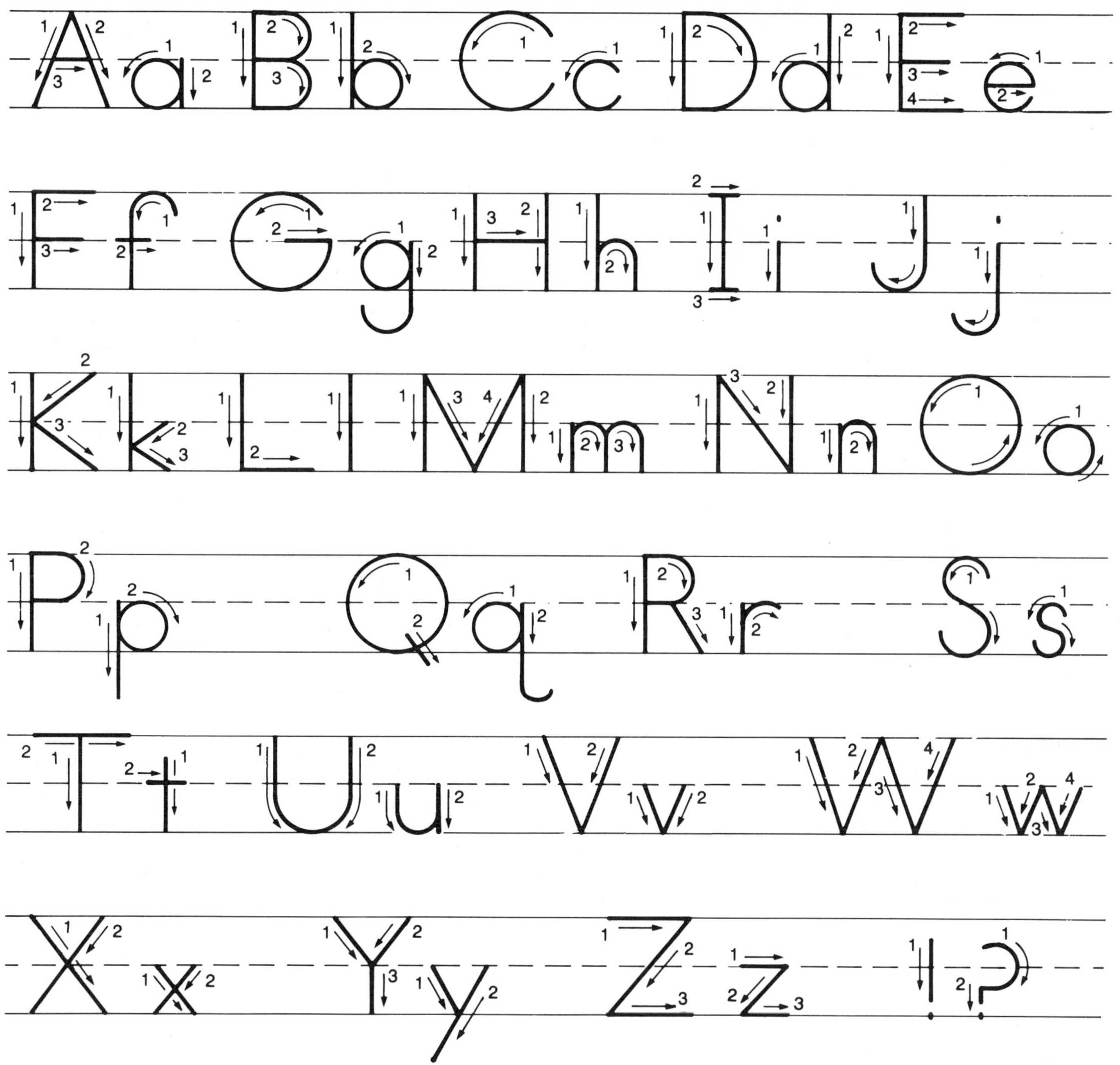

Appendix C

INDEX I

<h1 style="text-align:center">Index I (Continued)</h1>

Index I (Continued)

INDEX II

Index II (Continued)

Activity	Page